You Say

101 devotions on your identity in Christ

Emily Owen

First published 2025 by Authentic Media Limited,
PO Box 6326, Bletchley, Milton Keynes, MK1 9GG.
authenticmedia.co.uk

British Library Cataloguing in Publication Data
A catalogue record for this book is available from the British Library.
ISBN: 978-1-78893-437-4
978-1-78893-438-1 (e-book)

EU GPSR Authorised Representative
LOGOS EUROPE, 9 rue Nicolas Poussin, 17000, LA ROCHELLE, France
E-mail: Contact@logoseurope.eu

Cover design by Fresh Vision Design

Contents

Introduction

My 18-month-old niece saw herself in a mirror: 'Baby!'
I looked at the same reflection and saw 'Abigail', because I knew her name.
She and I had a different perspective on the same thing.

Could the same be true of us and God?

We look at ourselves and see negatives, damage, failings.
And God looks at the same thing – us – and sees us differently.
Sees us positively.
Sees us as we really are.

My facial nerve was damaged in surgery when I was 19 years old.
Damage in the mirror, if I even looked in the mirror.
Over time, helped by Abigail's 'Baby!', I have learned that mine is not the only perspective.

'Who am I to you?' Jesus asked his disciples in Mark 8:29.
What if we ask the same question back:
'Who am I to you?'

I look in the mirror.
I see useless.
I see rejected.
I see difficult.
I see inadequacy.
I see failure.
I see trying.
I see a burden.
Tears come.

My eyes move to the ground.
It's safer not to look.

Look with my eyes.
His voice is gentle.
Compassionate.
I recoil.
I don't want him looking at me.
I hide.
But he's not put off by my defences.

Look with my eyes.
He says it again.

'I don't know how,' I whisper,
as I raise my eyes to the mirror.

I see rejected.
I see chosen.

Is he looking where I'm looking?

I see difficult.
I see precious.

Is he looking at me?

I see useless.
I see loved.

I turn to him,
and follow his gaze
as it leads me to me.

Look with my eyes.
I begin to see me.

We are more than we see in the mirror.

Abigail didn't know her name, but she would learn to know it.

Perhaps we don't know some of the names God calls us.
But we can come to know . . .

Who am I to you?

1 SHIELDED

The word of the LORD came to Abram . . . 'Do not be afraid Abram. I am your shield, your very great reward.'
Genesis 15:1

At the end of Genesis 14, we read about Abram standing strong.
Refusing to break his promise to God.
All looks good.
He's riding a spiritual wave.
And what does God say?

Don't be afraid.

What? Abram's not afraid! Is he?

Maybe, from the outside, your spiritual life looks good.
Perhaps you lead worship at church, or preach, or help with the children's work.
Perhaps you volunteer, perhaps you've joined a homegroup.
Perhaps you attend church every week.
Your spiritual life looks good.
You're sorted.

But you know.

On the inside, where no one sees, things aren't so good.
You're anxious. You're exhausted. You're putting on a face.
God sees you.
He doesn't need to be told.
Don't be afraid.

And God gives the 'how' as well as the 'what'.
I'm your shield.
The word 'shield' here has connotations of 'a leader who protects'.[1]
A shield prevents bombardment.
And God says, **I'm your shield.**
Don't be scared, Abram.
I'm your shield.
I'm leading you.
I'm protecting you.
Anything that comes at you must go through me.
You're safe.

Look with my eyes. What do you see?

Shielded.

Father God, thank you that my fears don't scare you away. You stay, and you protect me. Help me to be faithful to you. I want to be. May I always grow closer to you. Amen.

2 STRONG

That is why, for Christ's sake, I delight in weaknesses, in insults, in hardships, in persecutions, in difficulties. For when I am weak, then I am strong.

2 Corinthians 12:10

Samson was strong.
Until he cut his hair.

God had forewarned that if Samson's hair was cut, Samson would lose his strength.
Samson's enemies tricked him into having his hair cut.
And his strength left him.

Samson allowed people to remove his source of strength.
Do you?
'God is our . . . strength' (Ps. 46:1).
Do we allow God to get pushed out, and sidelined?

Perhaps we become busy, or distracted, and we forget to plug into our Strength.
We allow it to be cut off.

Samson was captured, had his eyes gouged out, and put in prison.
'But the hair on his head began to grow again' (Judg. 16:22).
Having his hair cut didn't mean he'd lost his strength forever.
Just as taking our focus off God doesn't mean we'll stay that way forever.
With God, there is always a way back.

Perhaps, growing up strong, Samson had forgotten where his strength came from.
Perhaps, in our doing and our living, we forget who enables us.
'I can do all this through him who gives me strength.'[1]

In his weakness, Samson called out to God,
'Strengthen me. Please.'[2]

I can't do this myself.
I'm not strong.
I need your help.
Please strengthen me?
And God answered,
Yes.

Look with my eyes. What do you see?

Strong.

Father God, when I am weak, you are strong. Help me to welcome your strength in me. Amen.

3 INVITED

The Lord had said to Abram, 'Go from your country, your people and your father's household to the land I will show you.'

Genesis 12:1

'Would you like to come with me?'
When my niece was small, she'd often ask me this question.
Perhaps she'd been asked to change her clothes,
or read a book,
or tidy the playroom.
'Would you like to come with me?'
What she really meant was, 'I'd like you to come.'

When God says to Abram 'go', we might read it as an order.
Come on, Abram, quick march!
But, if we look at the root of the words, we see it is an invitation.
Would you like to come with me, Abram?
Would you like to see what I've got to show you?
It's not 'off you go', it's off *we* go.
In other words, **I'd like you to come. Will you?**
An invitation.
Would you like to come with me? I've got something to show you . . .

Abram would have to leave things behind.
He'd have to let them go.

I played the flute.
Then I lost my hearing.
I couldn't play anymore, but I held onto that flute for a long time.
God patiently encouraged me to let it go.
And when I finally did, my hands weren't holding it anymore.

They weren't clinging to what used to be.
They were open, ready to receive God's blessing.

Would you like to come with me?
I'd like you to.
I've got something to show you . . .

Look with my eyes. What do you see?

Invited.

Father God, yes please. I'd like to come with you. Help me to let go of things that get in the way. Open my eyes to things you have to show me today. Amen.

4

CARRIED

'I will make you into a great nation and I will bless you . . .'
Genesis 12:2

'Do it myself!'
Most people who have spent time with children will have been on the receiving end of this. And often, the children eventually must face the fact that they can't 'do it myself'.

Perhaps we never really grow out of the natural 'do it myself' mode we are born into.
As adults, a 'how to' instinct often comes to the fore.

Abram could have panicked:
Great nation? Me? Well, how's that going to happen? What does great nation even mean? I'd better look it up, so I can start planning.

But Abram didn't panic. And that meant he didn't miss two very important words.
'I will.'
I will make you into a great nation.
I will bless you.
When God says I will, he means it.
When God says I will, he means that we don't have to do it ourselves.
Because he will.

When I was on a life-support machine (before I lost my hearing), I needed to learn to breathe. I couldn't do it.
So my dad sat by my bed, and told me what to do.
'Breathe, breathe, breathe . . . '
I couldn't do it myself, and Dad stepped in.
All I had to do was stay with him.

God says, **I will.**
I will do it. I will help you breathe.
You're not on your own. Don't panic.
Everything is not on your shoulders.
It's on mine. I know you. I formed you. I'm right here.
And I will bless you.
I will.

Look with my eyes. What do you see?

Carried.

Father God, so often, I can't. I can't carry everything, I can't face tomorrow, I can't figure out what to do. I panic. In the storm, help me to hear your 'I will' promise, reminding me that I'm not alone. Amen.

5 UNINTERRUPTED

Then Melchizedek king of Salem brought out bread and wine. He was priest of God Most High, and he blessed Abram . . .

Genesis 14:18–19

The doorbell rang. I was busy. I left my study and invited the person in.

It was as I went to make them a cup of tea that God whispered to me:
With me, there are no interruptions.

Melchizedek seems to interrupt the narrative here.
Abram returns from defeating some kings, is met by the king of Sodom – a meeting which is apparently interrupted by Melchizedek – and then the king of Sodom continues the conversation, as though unaware that anything has happened.

But something has happened.
Melchizedek, king of Salem and priest of God Most High.

He brought out bread and wine, and blessed Abram.
Abram is probably battle-weary.
He's probably tired.
And he's met by Melchizedek.

Melchizedek, Hebrews 7 tells us, is a type/foreshadowing of Jesus.
In the aftermath of battle, Abram may well have been running on empty.
Unbeknown to him, the king of Sodom was about to try to persuade him to break a promise to God.[1]
And Melchizedek steps in.
Offering nourishment. Giving blessing. Offering his name.
King of Salem. King of peace.[2]

Maybe you're battle-weary. Will you let Jesus step in?
Offering nourishment. Giving blessing. Offering his name.
Prince of Peace.[3]

After the 'not-interruption', Abram strongly refused to break his promise to God.
Perhaps, without the 'not-interruption', he'd have wavered.
Let Jesus step in. He's not there to interrupt your life.
He's not there to spoil it, he's there to bless it.
He knows your life, and he's with you in it.
Your Prince of Peace.

Look with my eyes. What do you see?

Uninterrupted.

Father God, I welcome you. I'm sorry for times when other pressures push you out. May your presence be uninterrupted in my life. Please bless me, keep me, make your face smile on me, and give me your peace. Amen.

6 CENTRED

So Abram went, as the LORD had told him . . . and they set out for the land of Canaan, and they arrived there.

Genesis 12:4–5

Abram left.
He set off.
Inching towards Canaan, about 400 miles, on foot.
Not knowing where he was going, but following God anyway.
And then we have a key phrase: 'they arrived there.'

They arrived at the place God had promised to show them.
The place God knew they were going to, but they didn't know.
They arrived there.

Where are you at the moment?
Are you travelling, unsure of what is ahead?
God is keeping you company on the journey.
He knows where you're going.
You'll arrive there with him.

When Abram reached Canaan, he went right to Shechem, in the centre of the land.
All around were Canaanites.
Scary stuff.
God came and assured Abram that this was indeed the land God had earmarked for him.
And what did Abram do?
What's the first thing he did in this new land?
He built an altar to the Lord.
An act of worship, and of submission.

Abram was in a situation that was strange, that was difficult, that was alien and, right in the centre of it all, he reminded himself that God is God.

Do we welcome God into the midst of our difficulties, struggles, mess?
Abram could have built the altar on the outskirts, or hidden behind a hill.
Somewhere he might have felt less vulnerable.
But no. He welcomed God into the middle of his situation.
And God stayed.

Look with my eyes. What do you see?

Centred.

Father God, thank you for staying, even in my hard times. Thank you for keeping me company. Help me to recognise you at the centre of everything. I worship you. Amen.

7 BELOVED

No longer will you be called Abram; your name will be Abraham, for I have made you a father of many nations.

Genesis 17:5

My 4-year-old nephew had been at an event with me.
He'd heard 'Emily' said many times. After the event, he confided something; 'Lots of people call you "Emily", but I know your name is really Aunty Memem.'

Abram, which means 'exalted father' had his name changed to Abraham, 'father of many'.
God put a name to his 'great nation' promise made back in Genesis 12.

At this point Abraham had one son, and his wife was not the child's mother.
Hardly a great nation, yet God names Abraham 'father of many'.
One day, he would become that, yes, but he wasn't yet.

God looked at Abram, and saw the 'Abraham' God knew was in there.
Lots of people call you 'Abram', but I know your name is really Abraham.
Abraham struggled to believe it.[1]
He thought it was ridiculous.
How could he be Abraham?
Yet he was. Because God named him.

What do people call you?
Perhaps they define you by what you do, or by how you look.
Perhaps they put you down, or lay demands on you.
Perhaps they snatch your confidence, leaving you no room to just be.
What do you call you?
When you look in the mirror, who looks back?

What does God call you?
He calls you 'Beloved'.[2]
Lots of people call you x/y/z, but I know your name is really Beloved.

Maybe you struggle to believe it.
Maybe you think it's ridiculous.
How can you be Beloved?
Yet you are.
Because God named you.

Look with my eyes. What do you see?

Beloved.

Father God, thank you that you know my name. When I forget what I'm called, and other names crowd in, help me to listen for your voice, calling my real name – Beloved – over it all. Amen.

8 HIDDEN

Adam and his wife were both naked, and they felt no shame.
Genesis 2:25

Hiding. It's a natural response to things not being right, isn't it?
Maybe we've made a mistake.
Maybe things overwhelm us.
And we hide, to try to block those things out.

Genesis 2 gives the account of God creating Adam and Eve.
They were naked.
And they felt no shame.
They were fine with it.

How, then, did they end up hiding?
Not only hiding, but hiding from God himself?

Adam and Eve ate forbidden fruit, realised they were naked, and they panicked.
They were scared. So they hid.

God doesn't address their disobedience straight away.
He first addresses the consequences of it.
And we can sense God's pain.

Who told you you're naked?[1]
Who told you that being the you I made you to be was not enough?
Who made their words louder to you than my voice?
Who introduced you to shame?

This is the first time we read of people hiding, and it breaks God's heart.
It causes separation.
There's something between him and the people he loves.

Fast forward to Colossians, and we see the redemption of God.
He shows us how to truly hide.
Not *from* him, but *in* him.

Adam and Eve hid in fear. A scary place to be.

God hides us in love.
He surrounds us.
Anything that comes at us comes through a God-filter.
Hidden, not hiding, is a safe place to be.

Look with my eyes. What do you see?

Hidden.

Father God, I do hide from you. I know I do. I get scared and I hide. I want to be hidden in your love, not hide in my shame. Help me believe that it's safe to let you truly see me. Amen.

9

PRAISER

To bestow on them a crown of beauty instead of ashes, the oil of joy instead of mourning, and a garment of praise instead of a spirit of despair.

Isaiah 61:3

Have you ever had a despairing spirit?
Knowing God is there, but feeling that life is crashing down around you?
I have, and this verse is helpful, because it offers suggestions.
It does not say 'get a grip, pray more, go to church more, and your spiritual life will grow stronger'.
These things will help, but sometimes they are the next step.
We first need to stand, and get dressed.
Put on praise.

Maybe when we look through our wardrobe, praise is hiding at the back.
Push aside faint spirit clothes, and reach for praise anyway.

> Though the fig-tree does not bud . . . yet I will rejoice in the Lord . . .
>
> *Hab. 3:17–18*

Make a deliberate decision to praise.
Be determined to find something good, and thank God for it.
Beautiful tree? Thank you, Lord.
Someone offers help? Thank you, Lord.
Hospital bed has a comfy pillow? Thank you, Lord.

As we adopt a habit of praise, our spirits are strengthened in him.
We are reminded that he is in everything, and everything is in him.

When we feel spiritually faint, praise is our smelling salts.
Reviving us, reminding us that the joy of the Lord really is our strength.[1]

In Victorian Britain, police constables would carry smelling salts, so that they could revive fainting women.
A constable is a police officer of the lowest rank, yet carried something vital.

When we feel despairing and low, we can still carry something vital:
Praise.

Look with my eyes. What do you see?

Praiser.

Father God, help me to pick up my smelling salts and praise you today. Amen.

10

LISTENER

The LORD came and stood there, calling as at the other times, 'Samuel! Samuel!'
Then Samuel said, 'Speak, for your servant is listening.'

1 Samuel 3:10

This is the fourth time God called to Samuel.
The first three times, Samuel didn't know who was calling him.
And on the fourth time, he got it.

God wants us to hear him.
He didn't give up at the first attempt with Samuel.
And he won't give up with us.

God speaks, but perhaps we don't always recognise his voice.
We need to learn to listen.

Since losing my hearing, my way of listening to what people say is by lipreading.
In order to lipread, I have to look.
I don't always understand but, if I'm to have a chance, I need to look at people's lips.
To listen, I have to look.

> If you look for me wholeheartedly, you will find me.
>
> *Jer. 29:13,* NLT

As we look to God, as we spend time with him, being aware of him with us, we will see him more and more. And as we see him, we will hear his voice.

We will become God-listeners.

The word Samuel uses for 'listening' carries the meaning of listening in order to understand. Samuel wants to understand what God is saying.

I sometimes wish God would write his wishes clearly in the sky.
He could do that, but he doesn't.
What he does do is place within us the ability to hear him.
To listen and understand . . .

What will he say to you today?

Look with my eyes. What do you see?

Listener.

Father God, thank you that you speak. You want me to hear you. I want me to hear you. Help me learn to recognise your voice, and to become a God-listener. I'll start today . . . Amen.

STILL

The Lord will fight for you; you need only to be still.

Exodus 14:14

The Israelites have finally escaped Egypt and cruel Pharaoh, and they're camped by the sea. One day, word scurries through the camp:
'Pharoah's army is coming!'
Sea one side, approaching army on the other. Panic, panic, panic.
'We wish we were back in Egypt.'

The Israelites hated being in Egypt, yet the situation they were now in was so bad that they wished they were back there.
They couldn't fight for themselves.
They couldn't see a way out.
They panicked.
They cried out to God.
They had a go at Moses, who said,

> The Lord will fight for you; you need only to be still.

And God did fight for them.
He parted the sea, giving them a way out.
Perhaps you're in a situation and you can't see a way out.
You're exhausted, you're scared, you're running out of fight.
You don't know what to do.
If only someone would tell you.

I will fight for you. You need only to be still.

Let God tell you.
Let him fight for you, protect you, care for you.

You can do it.
Take a deep breath, and hear him say, 'Be still.'

I am God.
You know that.
So be still.[1]

Look with my eyes. What do you see?

Still.

Father God, please help me be brave enough to stop fighting, and to hand it over to you. You are God, I know that, so I can be still. I need to be still, deep inside me. Please help. Amen.

GLORY-REFLECTOR

When Moses came down from Mount Sinai with the two tablets of the covenant law in his hands, he was not aware that his face was radiant because he had spoken with the Lord.

Exodus 34:29

When the Israelites were still, when they focused on God rather than the approaching army, what happened? God got the glory:

> I will gain glory for myself . . .
>
> *Exod. 14:4b*

Are you someone who radiates Jesus?
Perhaps you don't know, and perhaps that's a good way to be.

Moses had no idea that he radiated the presence of God.
What he did know was that he'd spent time with God.
He'd spent deliberate time with God, he'd stilled himself before God.
And God's glory shone through.
I will gain glory for myself.
God is well able to glorify his name. Will he do so through you?

I remember a time, reading John 12, when I prayed Jesus' prayer for myself:

> Glorify your name!
>
> *John 12:28*

I knew what that meant. The surgery I was about to have would not paralyse me: I'd walk out of the hospital, and God would get the glory.
'Glorify your name.'

The surgery paralysed me. And during the months in hospital, God was glorified.
People came together in prayer for me.
In the hospital, I spoke of him with patients and staff.
In the mess of the hospital, God's glory was there.
In the panic of the approaching army, God's glory was there.
God was there.
For all to see.

God can promote his name.
Will he do so through us?
Be still . . .

Look with my eyes. What do you see?

Glory-reflector.

Father God, may your glory be seen in and through me. Amen.

13 ABLE

To these four young men God gave knowledge and understanding of all kinds of literature and learning. And Daniel could understand visions and dreams of all kinds.

Daniel 1:17

All eyes were on Daniel.
'Can you interpret my dream?' the king demanded.
'No . . .' A gasp rippled round the room.
This was Daniel. They knew Daniel could interpret dreams. So why was he saying no?
'. . . but God can.'
And God did, through Daniel.

Daniel was able to interpret the dream because he relied on God's ability, not his own.
He never lost sight of that.

Enabled by God.
It means saying, with John the Baptist, 'He must become greater' (John 3:30).
It means stepping back.
It means letting God get the glory.
It means letting him be bigger in your life.
It means enjoying being enabled by him.

In 1924, Eric Liddell won gold at the Olympics.
In the *Chariots of Fire* film about his life, his character said: 'God made me fast. And when I run, I feel his pleasure.'[1]
Liddell was good, and he never pretended he wasn't. No false humility for him, but true humility: he acknowledged he was good through God.

Daniel interpreted dreams. But only because God made him able.
Eric Liddell ran fast. But only because God made him able.
And I think Daniel, as well as Liddell, would have enjoyed feeling God's pleasure in them as they lived his enabling.

Do you enjoy it? Because you can.
Feel his pleasure in you.
Through God, you are able.

> Now may the God of peace . . . equip you with everything good for doing his will . . .
>
> *Heb. 13:20–21*

Look with my eyes. What do you see?

Able.

Father God, thank you that in you, I am able. I don't need to pretend I'm not good at things. Please help me share your pleasure in me. Amen.

KNOWN

For you created my inmost being; you knit me together in my mother's womb.

Psalm 139:13

'We'd like you to speak on Psalm 139.'
Outwardly, I agreed.
Inwardly, I balked.
I avoided Psalm 139, ever since I was 16 and diagnosed with tumours that swarm all over my body. Tumours that are genetic; with me since birth.

You mean, you knew? **Yes, I did.**
I don't like this psalm. **Right.**
I can't believe you knew. **Perhaps you'd prefer it if I didn't?**
Well, I . . . **Perhaps it would be better if neither of us knew?**
It might, actually. Then we'd be in it together. **In what?**
In not knowing what's ahead. **You want neither of us to know?**
Yes. No. I don't know. Are you glad you knew?
I am.
Why?
So that one of us knows, and you don't have to.

Will you trust my knowing?
Even when I don't understand it? **Even then.**
Even when I don't know myself?
In my knowing,
you are known.
I'm in your knowing? That's a reassuring place to be.
I don't want neither of us to know.

Do not be afraid of tomorrow, God is already there.
He recognises the 'you' who will meet him in tomorrow.
Scared you? Capable you? Riding a wave you? In the depths you? Tired you?

He recognises you in each aspect of yourself.

In his knowing,
you are known.

Look with my eyes. What do you see?

Known.

Father God, thank you for knowing me better than I know myself. You know what is ahead, so I don't have to just yet. Help me to trust your knowing. Amen.

SECURE

For you died, and your life is now hidden with Christ in God.
Colossians 3:3

My mum has a collection of Russian dolls.
Dolls which all have another doll hidden inside them.
I used to love working my way through from the biggest doll, eventually reaching a tiny doll which was smaller than my little finger.

At the time, I didn't connect the dolls with Colossians 3.
Then the carpet of my life was pulled from under me,
a shock health diagnosis,
surgeries which left me visibly different;
the foundations I hadn't realised I relied on crumbled.

I didn't feel safe in my life anymore.
Things were flying at me left, right and centre.

My life is hidden with Christ in God became a mantra, as I determined more and more not to lose sight of myself within a life that didn't look like mine.

Me surrounded by Christ surrounded by God felt – indeed, feels – a safe place to be.

Through this verse, God whispered to me; 'Anything and anyone that comes at you has to go through me first.'

That doesn't mean situations are easy.
It does mean they are less hard.

It doesn't mean they disappear.
It does mean they are less dominating.

It doesn't mean they don't hurt.
It does mean I'm hugged in the hurting.

> He knows the way I take . . .
>
> *Job 23:10*

And the same is true for you.

Look with my eyes. What do you see?

Secure.

Father God, whatever happens in my life, I'm safe with you. Help me not to doubt. You know the way I take. Amen.

16 LOVED

Jesus looked at him and loved him.

Mark 10:21a

My face was damaged in surgery. I didn't want anyone seeing me.
When I finally turned my face towards my mum, I saw only love.

You're walking along with Jesus, listening to him.
Footsteps come closer, a rhythmic beat of someone running.
It must be one of the children Jesus has just been talking to.
Annoyed, you glance over your shoulder.
And you see a man, running fast.
You can see his bare legs.
How embarrassing.
How shameful.
Doesn't he know anything about cultural etiquette?

You walk quicker, trying to hurry Jesus along, away from this man, but Jesus has stopped. He's turned to face the man, who runs right up to Jesus and falls on his knees.

You're about to step in, but you remember how well 'stepping in' went with the children.[1]

As you hesitate, the man speaks.
He wants to know how to have eternal life.
Jesus replies that the man knows the commandments.
'I've kept them all my life,' the man is still breathing hard.
You raise your eyebrows. Running and boasting. That won't go down well with Jesus.
You turn to Jesus, and your words freeze in your mouth.

He's looking straight at the sweaty, dishevelled, boasting man.
It's not a look of chastisement, or repulsion.
It's a look of pure love.
Agape love.[2]

> For I am convinced that [nothing] . . . will be able to separate us from the love of God that is in Christ Jesus our Lord.
>
> *Rom. 8:38–39*

Nothing.
Not looking a mess, feeling a mess, messing up.
Nothing can separate you from his love.

Look with my eyes. What do you see?

Loved.

Father God, When I don't love myself, help me to know that you do. And when I do love myself, remind me that you love me more. Thank you. Amen.

17

HEART-HEARD

You know what I long for, Lord; you hear my every sigh.
Psalm 38:9, NLT

The bleeding stopped.
Just like that, after twelve years.
The cause of her shame, and poverty, and isolation, and humiliation vanished.

Her money had – futilely – been spent on doctors. She had nowhere else to turn.
Everyone knew that Jesus could heal. He was her final hope. Yet she had no words.

How to articulate the longing in her heart?
How to again verbalise her desire to be made clean, risking more disappointment?

With a heart full of hoping, and a mouth empty of words, she snuck through the crowd.
'You shouldn't be here. You're unclean,' her head insisted.
According to the law, her head was right.
Yet she pressed on to get to Jesus, reaching out to touch his cloak, and the bleeding stopped. It was as though he'd known what her heart was asking for; not that he'd have noticed her among the crowd.

Trying to sneak away, Jesus' voice stopped her: 'Who touched me?' (Luke 8:45).
He had noticed her. Her heart had been heard.
And, through not running away, she'd let him see it.

He did know what her heart was asking for.
He knew her heart better than she did:

> Daughter . . . Go in peace . . .
>
> *Mark 5:34*

She'd become used to not belonging. Lack of peace was her norm. So much so that she didn't realise how much her heart needed peace. *Daughter . . . go in peace.*

Because of Jesus, things had changed, beyond what she'd hoped for.

> [He] is able to do immeasurably more than all we ask or imagine, according to his power that is at work within us . . .
>
> *Eph. 3:20*

Look with my eyes. What do you see?

Heart-heard.

Father God, thank you for hearing and understanding my heart's language, even when it doesn't have words. Amen.

18 SURROUNDED

'Don't be afraid,' the prophet answered. 'Those who are with us are more than those who are with them.'

2 Kings 6:16

The king of Aram is furious. He is at war with Israel yet, every time he makes an attack, it's as though someone has warned the king of Israel. He learns that there is indeed a someone.
Someone by the name of Elisha.

The king of Aram finds out where Elisha is – the city of Dothan – and sends an army to capture him.
The next morning Elisha and his servant see that the city is surrounded.
Elisha reassures his panicking servant, and asks God to open the servant's eyes.

Now the servant, as well as Elisha, can see an army of fire round Elisha.
They're surrounded by more than the king of Aram's army.
Just as we are surrounded by more than the 'armies' that come at us.

> For the angel of the LORD is a guard; he surrounds and defends all who fear him.
>
> *Ps. 34:7, NLT*

As the Aramite soldiers come towards Elisha, they are struck blind.
Elisha leads them to Samaria, where the king of Israel is, and advises the king not to kill them.
Instead, he suggests giving them food and water, before sending them back to Aram.

The king could have killed them, yet he moves from wanting to kill, to wanting to bless.

He prepares 'a great feast' (2 Kgs 6:23) for them, sending them back to their master when they've eaten. Subsequently, Aram stopped attacking Israel.

Blessing is a powerful thing.

Elisha moves from Dothan to Samaria.
He encounters blind armies and seeing armies.
He dares suggest blessing rather than hate.

And he does it all from 'surrounded'.

Look with my eyes. What do you see?

Surrounded.

Father God, when armies surround me, from inside and out, help me remember that you surround me closer. You defend and protect me from all else. Amen.

19

IMAGE-BEARER

So God created mankind in his own image, in the image of God he created them; male and female he created them.

Genesis 1:27

Queen Esther's people, the Jews, were being persecuted by Haman, and Esther was the only one in a position to help them.
She needed to speak to the king, but it was against the law for her to speak with him unbidden, and he hadn't asked to speak with her for the past thirty days.[1]
Risking death, Esther prepared herself to appear before the king.
She put on her royal robes, she stood in the king's court, and she waited.

The king saw her.
Perhaps her heart beat quicker as she stood, waiting.
The king held out his hand towards her.
His hand was holding a golden sceptre.
Holding out the golden sceptre meant 'welcome'.

The king saw Esther.
He saw her standing there, dressed in royal robes.
Robes he himself had given her.
Robes that showed she belonged to the royal household.
The Royal Family.
And he was pleased with her.

The king saw his own mark, his royalty, on Esther.
He'd given her royal robes, she was wearing them, and that gave him joy.

God has put his own mark on us.
His 'image' (Gen. 1:27).
And if God made everyone in his image, his image is in you.
God sees his image in you.
He's pleased to see his image in you.
He put it there on purpose.

I'm made in your image!
Your image is in me!
We're related!
Give me identity and belonging that come from you.
Give me joy in us.

Look with my eyes. What do you see?

Image-bearer.

Heavenly Father, I'm shy to ask, but where do you see your image in me? Can we look for it together? Amen.

20 RECOGNISED

Come near to God and he will come near to you.

James 4:8

The man watched his son walk away, walking tall, dressed in fine clothes.
The family weren't short of a penny or two.
The man was devastated.
His son, the boy he had nurtured, provided for, watched grow, was leaving.

When his son had asked for his inheritance, the man had been surprised.
It was an unusual request.
People didn't receive inheritance until the giver had died.
Did his son wish him dead?
His son disappeared over the horizon.
The man watched the way his son had gone, and he kept watching.

The son arrived in a far-flung place and had a great time.
Until the cash ran out.
At the same time, the country was consumed by famine.
No money, and no food to buy if there had been.
The son got himself a job feeding pigs. So embarrassing.[1]
How had it come to this?
The pigs had more food than he did.
The son caught himself wishing he could eat the pigs' food.
Maybe he should go home.
But he'd treated his dad so badly.

The man watched the way his son had gone.
A figure appeared on the horizon, stooping, dirty, dressed in rags.
Hesitance in every step.
And the man ran.
Not away but towards.

The son was in a hard place, yet his dad still recognised him.
However much things change, God recognises us.
Even when we don't recognise ourselves.
He watches for us.
He wants us to come home.
There is always a way back.

Look with my eyes. What do you see?

Recognised.

Father God, thank you that you watch for me. Help me to take that first step closer to you. Help me to come back. Amen.

ALLOWED

Why this waste of perfume? It could have been sold for more than a year's wages and the money given to the poor.

Mark 14:4–5

It seems a fair question.
After all, it was customary to give money to the poor on the eve of Passover.

The group had been having dinner when a woman appeared with a jar of perfume, pouring it on Jesus' head. An act of worship and devotion. An act that was allowed by Jesus.

We know that Jesus cared about the poor. We know he did, and his followers and disciples would have been encouraged to do the same. Yet he welcomes the woman's gift to him:

> Leave her alone . . . She has done a beautiful thing to me.
>
> *Mark 14:6*

Sometimes, no matter how much 'helping the poor' we are engaged in, it's good to remind ourselves of why we are doing it.
The woman put Jesus first. In this moment, he was her sole focus and, rather than telling her to go and see to the poor, he welcomed it.
He allowed her to put him first.

Is he asking you to make time for him?
Listen for his 'Leave her alone' defending you against voices that may suggest you're not allowed.
Jesus welcomes your presence. He calls it a beautiful thing.

The woman put him first, despite the other people around her.
She may have served at the dinner, helping others.
There were probably more jobs she could have been getting on with.
And Jesus allowed her to also shift her focus solely onto him.

> [Jesus] said to them, 'Come with me by yourselves to a quiet place . . . '
>
> *Mark 6:31*

Where's your quiet place with him?
You're allowed to go there.
Allowed by Jesus.

Look with my eyes. What do you see?

Allowed.

Father God, thank you for opportunities to serve. Thank you for opportunities to just be with you. Sometimes I am better at serving. Help me remember I'm allowed time by myself with you, too. Amen.

PART

[Jesus said] 'I am the vine; you are the branches. If you remain in me and I in you, you will bear much fruit; apart from me you can do nothing.'

John 15:5

Come and see my vineyard.
Raising your hand to shield your eyes from the sun, you follow him.
Reaching the top of a hill, you see the vineyard in the distance.
It's big.
He must have lots of vines.
Reaching the vineyard, you push branches aside, looking for the vines.
Why are there no vines?

Come and see my vineyard.
He beckons you further in.
You come to a vine. It's the only vine.
All the branches come from it.
He knows all their names.

Come and see my vineyard.
He's inviting you to look closer.
You examine the vine, you examine the branches.
You're not sure where the branches end or where the vine starts.
You check as many branches as you can.
He sees where you're looking.
You turn to look at him.

Come and see my vineyard.
He runs his hand along the branch and onto the vine.
Then he holds his hand out to you.
You take it, and you begin to understand.

Imagine being so close to Jesus as you live that it is hard to see where one starts and the other ends. You're part of him.
Imagine that you don't need to imagine, because you know.

Apart from him, we can do nothing. A part of him, we can do everything.

Look with my eyes. What do you see?

Part.

Father God, sometimes I try to go it alone. In those times, please help me to remember how close you are. I want to be in a place that I can't see where I end and you start; a part of you. Amen.

LIT

Therefore, if anyone is in Christ, the new creation has come: the old has gone, the new is here!

2 Corinthians 5:17

'The old was gone, but it isn't gone anymore, because it's come back.' That's not what the verse says, but how often is it what we make the verse say? Negative things that we've said, or done, or experienced, refuse to 'stay gone'.

'New creation' is singular in the Greek. New *creature* has come. When we turn to Christ, we are individually made new.

2 Corinthians was written by the apostle Paul, who once made it his life's work to persecute Christians. And then came Damascus . . .

> As [Paul] neared Damascus on his journey, suddenly a light from heaven flashed around him.
>
> *Acts 9:3*

God clicked his fingers. **OK, Paul, the old has gone.**
And God literally switched on the light. Click.

Paul's new creation began with light. Just as the creation of the world began with light.[1] Just as our new creation – our new creature – begins with light.[2]

Paul went on to make and encourage Christians.
Despite his past, Paul was genuine when he wrote 'the old has gone'.
He'd met with God. He'd let go. 'Let there be light' (Gen. 1:3).

The old was often remembered and always gone.

Sometimes, darkness is tempting. Paul would have known advantages in his old life, yet he could write that Christ was more:

> But whatever were gains to me I now consider loss for the sake of Christ.
>
> *Phil. 3:7*

The old had gone. Let there be light. Paul's life lit up.
And light begins with Jesus.

Look with my eyes. What do you see?

Lit.

Incidentally, 'Lit' in modern slang means excellent . . .

Father God, when I met you, my life lit up. Help me to remember that your light does not fade. I don't need to go back to darkness. I can walk in your Light, every day. Every day lit. Amen.

24 EQUIPPED

For the jar of flour was not used up and the jug of oil did not run dry, in keeping with the word of the LORD spoken by Elijah.
1 Kings 17:16

'I can't do this anymore,' mutters the woman to herself.
Famine was not unusual in Zarephath.
Each one was a struggle, more so since her husband died.
The woman has just had enough.
Stooping down, she picks up another stick.

A voice startles her: 'Will you get me a drink?'
Wordlessly, the woman goes to get some water, but the voice stops her: 'And some bread, please.'
That's too much.
'I don't have any bread. I only have a little flour and oil, which I'm going home to cook. After that, there's nothing. My son and I will die.'

Elijah's request for food didn't surprise the widow.
She'd been told by God to feed him.[1]
Yet she has nothing.
How can she feed him?
Her reflex response is: 'I can't.'
She looks at the evidence – or lack of – and says, 'I can't.'

Even though God had told her to, she says *I can't.*
Maybe she is you.
Maybe she is me.

‘Don’t be afraid,’ says Elijah (v. 13).
You can do this.
God will give you more.
You will always have enough.

So the woman takes a risk. She makes a cake for Elijah. And the food doesn’t run out.[2]

Don’t be afraid.
I can do this.
God will give me more.
I will always have enough.

Look with my eyes. What do you see?

Equipped.

Father God, thank you that you equip me with all I need. Sometimes I don’t feel equipped for my life; help me to remember that in you, I am. I will always have enough. Amen.

POEIMA

For we are God's handiwork, created in Christ Jesus to do good works, which God prepared in advance for us to do.
Ephesians 2:10

Octavio Paz won the Nobel Prize for Literature in 1990. He said, 'The purpose of poetry is to restore to mankind the possibility to wonder.'[1]

We are God's handiwork – *poeima* – God's poem.
What are the good works he's prepared for us to do?
They will vary, but perhaps they meet in Paz's words:
To restore to mankind the possibility to wonder.

Romans 1:20 uses the same word – *poeima* – when talking about creation.
God's creation-poem restores to us the possibility of wonder.
We stand in awe at the starry sky, or majestic mountains.

What about his us-poem?
Do our lives, and things we do and say, lead people to wonder about God, and to wonder at God? Leading them to ask, is it possible that God . . .?

What about his you-poem? Do things in you cause you to wonder about and at God?
Sometimes, life can become so busy and routine that we forget about the possibility of wonder that is all around.
Help from a stranger, a hug from a child, sunshine . . . God is there.

Poetry is poetry. Whether rhyming, clashing, rhythmic, free-fall, long, short, it's possible to see poetry in everything. Even the despairing student, huddled over an indecipherable sonnet, doesn't refute that it's poetry.

God has declared us his *poeima*.
Different styles come and go, yet our identity as his poem remains.
Even on the days we are the despairing one, huddled over our indecipherable situations, we are still God's poetry.

If something is poetic, it has beauty and expression.
May God's *poeima* in and around you cause you to wonder and to worship.

Look with my eyes. What do you see?

Poeima.

Father God, please restore in me the possibility of wonder. I never want to take you or your *poeima* in and around me for granted. Amen.

CHILD

For I am the LORD your God who takes hold of your right hand and says to you, Do not fear; I will help you.

Isaiah 41:13

I was on holiday with my family.
As we waited to cross a road, I felt a hand slip into mine.
It was my 8-year-old niece.
'You're my adult.'
You'll look after me. You'll lead the way.
You'll tell me when it's safe to cross.
You're my adult.

She didn't try to lead the way.
She left that to me.
Because I was her adult.

Who's the adult in your relationship with God? Who leads the way?

> See what great love the Father has lavished on us, that we should be called children of God! And that is what we are!
>
> *1 John 3:1*

Our child-status before God is something we receive because he loves us so much.
He chooses to call us his children.

Our child-status doesn't mean we can't achieve, think, use our gifting.
Once we'd crossed the road, my niece pulled me towards a particular shop.
She knew where she wanted to go.
But, had there been reason to stop her, I could easily have done so.
Because our hands were joined.

Being God's child means going through life handheld by God himself. He holds your hand because he loves you and wants you safe.
Will you hold his hand back?

He'll look after you. He'll lead the way.
He'll tell you when it's safe to cross.
He's your adult.

Look with my eyes. What do you see?

Child.

Father God, thank you for being my adult. Help me to hold your hand as I go through life, so that you can gently pull me back when I need it. And I will need it! Thank you. Amen.

27

RIGHTEOUS

God made him who knew no sin to be sin for us, that in him we might become the righteousness of God.

2 Corinthians 5:21

'Don't tell her off, tell me off!'
I hated seeing my little sister cry.
Even when she'd been naughty, I wanted to be told off instead of her.
My parents never did. They couldn't.

'Don't look on their sin, make me be sin instead,' said Jesus.
And God did. He could.
So Jesus went to the cross.

Being covered by Jesus' blood makes us righteous.
Justified. 'Just as if I'd never sinned', as I learned in Sunday school.
When God looks at us, he sees Jesus.
He sees his righteousness.[1]

'Moses, what's in your hand?' God asks in Exodus 4:2.
'A staff' is the answer.
God would use Moses' staff in parting the Red Sea and in bringing water from a rock.[2]

But the staff wasn't amazing by itself.
The staff foreshadowed the cross.

The cross by itself wasn't amazing; Jesus made it so.
On the cross, he bought for us the righteousness of God.

I have a holding cross. It belonged to a friend who passed away from cancer, and is one of my most precious possessions.
My friend held onto the cross.
She couldn't do more.
She didn't need to do more.
She grasped the place where she was made righteous in God's sight.

> Then he said, 'Jesus, remember me when you come into your kingdom.'
> *Luke 23:42*

Look with my eyes. What do you see?

Righteous.

Father God, thank you for making it possible to look on me and see righteous. I know I mess up, and get things wrong. All I can do is hold onto the cross where I am made righteous. It's all I need to do. Help me hold on. Amen.

28 PEACE-FULL

May there be peace within your walls . . .

Psalm 122:7a

Many of us have walls in life.
Walls we build to get through the day, to keep people out, to prevent people seeing in.
Walls of structure, routine, things we need to do day in, day out.
Is there peace inside our walls?

Ephesians 6:15 encourages us to put on peace-shoes: 'Feet fitted with the readiness that comes from the [good news] of peace'.
The meaning in this passage is military.
Roman soldiers would wear protective, supportive foot gear, specifically designed for the soldier's lifestyle.

Our peace-shoes are specifically designed for our lifestyle as Christians.
Wherever we go, whatever our battles, we have peace – if we remember to put our shoes on.

There's something else that's special about being given peace-shoes to wear: they show belonging.
Every time a soldier looked at the shoes on his feet, he'd be reminded that he belonged in the army.

Perhaps we sometimes feel that we don't belong in the family of God.
What's on your feet?

> The runaway son returns.
> His father says, 'Quick, give him some shoes.'[1]
> Slaves went barefoot. Shoes denoted family, belonging.
> The son would have known relief at being given shoes.

> He belonged. He wasn't the slave he assumed he'd be.
> He'd expected to go barefoot, and his father thought him worthy of shoes.
> Looking at his feet would have brought peace.
> 'Quick, give him some shoes.'
> All the son had to do was put them on.

Perhaps you expect to go barefoot. You've become used to lack of peace.

God thinks you're worthy of peace. *Quick, give him some shoes.*

What's on your feet?

Look with my eyes. What do you see?

Peace-full.

Father God, may there be peace within my walls. Thank you for my peace-shoes; please help me remember to put them on. Amen.

SHINY

Do not conform to the pattern of this world, but be transformed by the renewing of your mind. Then you will be able to test and approve what God's will is . . .

Romans 12:2

Mr Happy and Mr Tickle decide to teach their grumpy pal a lesson.
They secretly follow him around and, every time he's grumpy, Mr Tickle tickles him.
At the end of the day, Happy tells Grumpy that if he were less grumpy, he wouldn't feel the weird tickle that had been following him all day.[1]

The implication here is that Grumpy can't control the tickles themselves but, by working on his grumpiness, the tickles will lessen by default.

> Do everything without grumbling or arguing, so that you may become blameless and pure, 'children of God without fault in a warped and crooked generation.' Then you will shine among them like stars in the sky as you hold firmly to the word of life.
>
> *Phil. 2:14–16*

Paul wrote these words.
Paul himself grumbled at times.
So what's going on?
Why did Paul veto grumbling?

If we look closer at the word translated 'grumbling', it means to secretly chunter away inside.
It's *that* that Paul says, 'don't do'.
Check your attitude.

Why? So that you may become pure, meaning 'not mixed with evil'.[2]
Paul doesn't say, 'Evil is all around, so lock yourself away, have no contact with anyone.'
He says, 'Evil is all around, so check inside.'

Similarly, the word he uses for 'arguing' means the thinking of a man deliberating with himself, inward reasoning. It doesn't mean having an argument with someone else.
Check inside.

We can't always control what happens around us, or inside us.
But perhaps,
if we keep our inside in check with Jesus,
we will begin to shine like stars.

Look with my eyes. What do you see?

Shiny.

Father God, I do grumble sometimes. Help me to bring you into my inside, help me check my attitude. Help me shine like stars with you. Amen.

30

UNASHAMED

'Then neither do I condemn you,' Jesus declared. 'Go now and leave your life of sin.'

John 8:11b

I'm used to men.
Men dragged me here. Everyone looking.
I'm used to men.

'What shall we do with her?' they ask the man called Jesus.
Huh. Men have never had a problem knowing what to do with me.
'We caught her in the act of adultery.'
I look at the ground, defiantly. I can't deny it.
I'm used to men.

He bends and writes on the ground. He says nothing.
I should have known better than to hope he'd defend me.
I'm used to men.

They want to stone me.
He straightens up. I look at the ground.
I'm used to men.

'Whoever has no sin can throw the first stone.'
He writes on the ground again. I wait for the stones.
I'm used to men.

No one is here. They've all walked away. Except Jesus.
He probably wants to stone me himself.
I'm used to men.

He stands. 'Where are they? Does no one condemn you?'
I shake my head.
'I don't condemn you, either.'

I thought I'd stopped feeling. I thought my heart was bullet-proof.
'I don't condemn you.'
His words are the stones, shattering my layers of protection, reaching me deep inside.
Beckoning life beyond existence.
'I don't condemn you.'

I'm not used to this man.

Look with my eyes. What do you see?

Unashamed.

Father God, you look at me, you see all that I am, yet you don't condemn me. Help me not to condemn myself. Thank you that you never walk away. Amen.

31

HYDRATED

The LORD is my shepherd . . . he leads me beside quiet waters, he refreshes my soul.

Psalm 12:1–3

Jesus was at the Feast of Tabernacles.
About 1,800 years before, the Israelites were wandering in the desert.
Once a year, they now took time to remember, by going to Jerusalem and living in tents for a week.

The Feast of Tabernacles had a party atmosphere.
Everyone was rejoicing, and celebrating; expectant, believing that the Messiah would come. They longed, as they had in the desert, for refreshment.

Each day began with a water-drawing ritual.
A priest would lead a joyful procession to draw water from Jerusalem's only water source. He'd plunge a gold pitcher into the water, and recite:
'With joy you will draw water from the wells of salvation' (Isa. 12:3).

The final day was most exciting of all.
The Great Praise Day.
A hush fell, the people listened to the wind, expressing their longing for spiritual refreshment.

It was into this, that Jesus made an extraordinary announcement:

> If anyone is thirsty, let him come to me and drink.
>
> *John 7:37, NIV 1984*

The people were thirsty, looking for refreshment.
They'd heard the recitation every day for a week.
They were expectant for the Messiah.
What they sought was right in front of them, and yet they missed it.

Soon, Living Water would be hanging on a cross.
Living Water would thirst.
They didn't come to him, they pushed him away, and so they didn't allow him to hydrate them. Didn't let him refresh their weary souls.

With joy you will draw water from the wells of salvation.
Will you?
Come to me . . .
Don't miss out.
Jesus' 'anyone' includes you.

Look with my eyes. What do you see?

Hydrated.

Father God, I am dehydrated. I need your Living Water. Thank you for inviting me to come to you and be refreshed. I'm coming. Amen.

SIBLING

For God knew his people in advance, and he chose them to become like his Son, so that his Son would be the firstborn among many brothers and sisters.

Romans 8:29, NLT

'I'll get my brother on to you!'
These words were used as a threat during playground dramas when I was at school.
It was the ultimate triumph: 'My brother will sort this out.'
Sometimes the words were directed at me.
I had no comeback, even if I'd been brave enough to make one.
I didn't have a brother.

People no longer tell me 'I'll get my brother on to you', I'm pleased to say, but perhaps I could say it to myself?
I do have a brother.
His name is Jesus.

What about when 'playground drama' equivalents happen now?
Feeling inadequate?
I'll get my brother onto you.
Inner voices telling you you're worthless?
I'll get my brother onto you.
Someone putting you down?
I'll get my brother onto you.

I do have a brother. So do you. His name is Jesus.

> If anyone causes one of these little ones – those who believe in me – to stumble, it would be better for them to have a large millstone hung round their neck and to be drowned in the depths of the sea.
>
> *Matt. 18:6*

How dare you, says our big brother. **How dare you get at my sibling. Not on my watch.**

Next time things get at you, tell them: 'I'll get my brother onto you.'
And you can be sure he'll be there.
You do have a brother.

His name is Jesus.

Look with my eyes. What do you see?

Sibling.

Lord Jesus, thank you for being my big brother. Thank you for defending me, and protecting me, and being there. Amen.

33

REDEEMED

With your unfailing love you lead the people you have redeemed.
In your might, you guide them to your sacred home.

Exodus 15:13, NLT

Putting my flute in its case for the last time, I gave it to a friend.
I couldn't play it anymore.
I needed to let go of my hearing-self of yesterday.

A couple of decades went past and I rarely saw this friend, touching base with her occasionally on social media.
Then my niece wanted to learn to play the flute.
A plan began to form in my mind.
Wouldn't it be lovely if she could learn on my flute?
But I didn't know if my friend still played it, nor was it any longer mine.

It turned out that she did still play, but was happy to let my niece have the flute.
So I bought it back.
My friend didn't only say she was happy, she said that the whole thing felt redemptive.

Don't be scared. I've redeemed you!
You're mine.
I know you sometimes stray. I'll bring you back.
Don't be scared.
I've redeemed you. I've bought you back.
I didn't get you for free; I bought you.
You. Personally. Are. Redeemed.
By me. You're mine.

You weren't a giveaway.
You weren't a 'buy one get one free'.
You weren't a 'two for one'.
You weren't an afterthought.
You were on my shopping list from the start.
I bought you.
You're worth it.
And so I paid for you.
Thorns, nails, cross.
I've redeemed you.
Because I wanted to.
You're mine.

Look with my eyes. What do you see?

Redeemed.

Father God, thank you for redeeming me. Amen.

34

ACCEPTED

Let your light shine before others, that they may see your good deeds and glorify your Father in heaven.

Matthew 5:16

It seems so easy for them. They just go up to Jesus. Why can't I do that?
I have so many questions. I tried, the other day.
He's in Jerusalem, and I tried, but what would my Pharisee colleagues think?
They were livid when Jesus cleared everyone out of the temple.
Between you and me, I wonder if he was right. I can't go up to Jesus.

People had flocked to Jesus,[1] seen the miracles and believed in him.
Nicodemus saw the miracles, too, and had questions.
Under cover of night, he went to Jesus.
And Jesus accepted him.
He discussed with Nicodemus in a way he hadn't with the crowds.[2]
Because Nicodemus' needs were different.

In John 7, Nicodemus' colleagues are determined to condemn Jesus, and Nicodemus suggests giving Jesus a fair hearing.
In John 19, Nicodemus, along with Joseph, buries Jesus. Not only that, he takes along enough myrrh and aloes as would have been used in a royal burial.
Nicodemus proclaims through his actions that Jesus is King.
What do our actions proclaim about Jesus?

Nicodemus' public honouring of Jesus began with being accepted in private.
It began with him daring to go to Jesus.
It began with him plucking up his courage; risking rejection but meeting acceptance.

Sometimes we look at others. It seems so easy for them – worshipping, serving, praising – and we feel like Nicodemus; wanting to join in but stuck.
Come as you are.
Accepted by Jesus.
Live in that acceptance.
And see where it takes you.

Let *your* light shine . . .

Look with my eyes. What do you see?

Accepted.

Father God, thank you that you accept me as I am. I don't need to be like anyone else. Help me to live accepted, and help my life to bring glory to you. Amen.

35

FORGIVEN

I have swept away your offences like a cloud, your sins like the morning mist. Return to me, for I have redeemed you.
Isaiah 44:22

We don't know what was said during the private conversation between Jesus and Peter.
We know what happened before it: Peter denied all knowledge of Jesus.[1]
We know what happened after it: Peter was asked to encourage others in Jesus.[2]
But we don't know what happened during it.

I'm glad we don't know.
Jesus can keep secrets.
Perhaps Jesus appeared to Peter and said, 'Come on, let's sort this out.'
They had a conversation.
They dealt with it, and they moved on.

The next time we read of them, Peter is leaping out of a boat to get to Jesus, and Jesus is welcoming him over breakfast.
No mention of the conversation that had put things right, because it had put things right.
Peter was forgiven.
Jesus can keep secrets.

I admire Peter.
He lived in the truth of forgiveness.
He's not rushing up to Jesus to say, 'I'm sorry about that thing I said.'
He's rushing to see Jesus, full stop.

He's living the truth of forgiveness.

Living in the truth of Jesus' forgiveness means believing that it's true. When we re-apologise, he says, **What are you talking about?**
We dealt with that.
Let's move on.

Jesus can keep secrets.
Have a chat with him,
deal with it,
and live in the truth of forgiveness.
Rush to see Jesus . . .

Look with my eyes. What do you see?

Forgiven.

Father God, you are a great secret-keeper. Help me to trust you with the secret things on my heart, so that there is nothing between us. I want to share with you, even when I have messed up. I'm rushing to see you. Amen.

JOY-FULL

Jesus said to her, 'Mary.' She turned toward him and cried out in Aramaic, 'Rabboni!' (which means 'Teacher').

John 20:16

Joy is one of my favourite words.
When things are difficult, I can't hand on heart say I'm happy.
I'm not always happy. But I do always know joy.

I'd just been told I needed surgery that would leave me deaf. A fairly rubbish day.
And it was raining. Then I saw a rainbow.

Mary is looking for Jesus.
She's crying. Turning away from the empty grave, she sees someone.
I'll ask the gardener: 'Sir, tell me where he is.'
And Someone speaks: 'Mary.'
Tear-filled eyes widen: 'Rabboni!'
He's there.

Through her tears, Mary saw Jesus. Through the rain, I saw rainbows.

> Despite the grey day, the bad news I'd received, the dread of more brain surgery and a silent future, the rainbows were there. I still look for rainbows: A smile from a baby, chocolate, a lunch date with a friend, a letter in the post. Anything that brightens my day.
> I find the rainbows. And I cling on.[1]

What do you see through your tears?

I have learned to see joy. Mary learned to see Jesus.
Where there is joy, there is Jesus.
Where there is Jesus, there is joy.
Joy is possible.
If we recognise Jesus in everyday joys – flowers, hugs, chocolate – and bring him into them, we will see him more and more.

> You make known to me the path of life; you will fill me with joy in your presence, with eternal pleasures at your right hand.
>
> *Ps. 16:11*

Look with my eyes. What do you see?

Joy-full.

Father God, thank you for joy. As I deliberately look for joy-moments, may I see and know you more and more. Amen.

INSEPARABLE

No, in all these things we are more than conquerors through him who loved us.

Romans 8:37

Growing up, my sister and I were inseparable. Mostly because we were good friends, and also mostly because I was a scaredy-cat. 'I'll go if Sophie comes too,' was my frequent refrain.
The places I was asked to go to weren't bad: a shop, or a party.
Still, 'I'll go if Sophie comes too.'

But the recipients of the letter to the church in Rome faced much harder things.
'Trouble . . . hardship . . . persecution . . . famine . . . nakedness . . . danger . . . sword' (Rom. 8:35) were their normal.

Paul, in his letter, poses the question,
'Who shall separate us from the love of Christ?'
Perhaps the church in Rome were beginning to wonder if God really loved them, given that they were having such a tough time.
Perhaps you wonder if God really loves you.
Perhaps you're having a tough time physically, emotionally, spiritually.
Who – or what – shall separate you from the love of Christ?

Paul's answer is emphatic: nothing.
Whatever you go through, you are inseparable from the love of Christ.
You're a more-than-conqueror.

If we are more than conquerors, what lies beyond?

The love of God that is in Christ Jesus our Lord.

Rom. 8:39

The love that nothing can separate us from. The love that, no matter what we go through, is with us and is waiting for us on the other side.

We don't only have victory in our situations, we have victory over and above and beyond them. Because nothing can separate us from his love.

I'm scared. Will you come too?
Yes. We're inseparable, you and I.

Look with my eyes. What do you see?

Inseparable.

Father God, help me to remember that 'nothing'. Nothing can take me away from your love. Wherever I go, whatever I do, or feel, or say; nothing. When I question, please remind me of nothing. Amen.

HOLY

Before I formed you in the womb I knew you, before you were born I set you apart; I appointed you as a prophet to the nations.

Jeremiah 1:5

From the beginning, God knew us.
The essence of who we are was there right from the start, and it still is.
You were planned in by God, written in to his creation long before he formed you in the womb.
You have always been known by God.
Recognised by him. Understood by him.
Set apart by him. Consecrated. Made holy.

Before the creation of the world, there was the essence of you and me that God set apart to be holy.

I've had many surgeries over the years. I have a condition called NF2 and, in my memoir, I wrote a letter to NF2:

> I know . . . there will be more days when I am surrounded by the shipwreck you make of my life . . . I will be clinging to a piece of me within that shipwreck. 'Emily' will still be there, wherever you take me.[1]

What if we change NF2 for life in general:
I know there will be days when I'm surrounded by mess.
Mess of my making, of others' making, of life.
On those days, especially on those days, I will cling to the holiness in me.
The holiness put there by God.
The holiness that nothing can take away.
God says so.

He made me. He knows me. He set me apart.
The holiness in me transcends all else.
Because God is there.

> Even before he made the world, God loved us and chose us in Christ to be holy and without fault in his eyes.
>
> *Eph. 1:4, NLT*

Look with my eyes. What do you see?

Holy.

Father God, thank you for placing holiness in me. You are there. Help me hold on tight. I choose holiness. I choose you. Amen.

39

GOD'S PLACE

Do you not know that your bodies are temples of the Holy Spirit, who is in you, whom you have received from God?
1 Corinthians 6:19

'My place or yours?' People might say this when arranging to meet.
What about God's place?

King Solomon built the temple. It took seven years.
On completion, Solomon called the Israelites to the temple to celebrate.[1]
Huge crowd outside, priests inside. Musicians played instruments, singing and praising and giving thanks to God.
Then the music stops.
They can't play anymore; cloud is filling the temple.
The 'glory of the LORD' (2 Chr. 5:14).
Glory so present that it obliterates all else.

The musicians would play again, praising and worshipping God, but for a time they were to simply make space for his glory, allowing his glory to speak for itself.
The temple was used for many good things. Sacrifices, worship, offerings, meetings.
And still there came a time when God said, 'Stop for a bit.'
Just be in my glory.

Maybe your life is full of good things; volunteering, serving, work.
In all those things, you are his temple, his dwelling place.
Do you make space for his glory? Time to just be in his glory?

Maybe you don't feel like somewhere God dwells; the idea that Almighty God would choose to have his Spirit living in you seems ridiculous.
Do you not know?
Don't you realise that your body is somewhere God chooses to be?
Don't you realise that in you is God's place?
That you *are* God's place?

Take time to realise.
To stand in awe.
To welcome God's glory.
To be in his presence.
To let his glory speak for itself.
Let the music of service fade, just for a bit . . .

Look with my eyes. What do you see?

God's place.

Father God, when you say, 'Shall we spend time at my place?', may I always say yes. And when I ask, 'Can we go to your place?', may I know that you always say yes. Amen.

40

BECOMING

And we all, who with unveiled faces contemplate the Lord's glory, are being transformed into his image with ever-increasing glory, which comes from the Lord, who is the Spirit.
2 Corinthians 3:18

Have you ever noticed that as people get older, they can increasingly resemble their parents? 'You're so like your mum/dad' is a phrase I often find myself thinking or saying.

If someone said to you, 'I see Jesus in you', what would your reaction be?
Perhaps a shrinking back, embarrassment, unsure how to respond.
But isn't that what we should be aiming for?
For people to look at us and see Jesus?
Just as we physically grow to resemble our parents, shouldn't we spiritually grow to resemble our Father?

I know few – if any – who decide to deliberately try to look like their parents.
It almost imperceptibly happens as they grow.
Of course there will be 'learned behaviours' that mark similarities, too.

> The fruit of the Spirit is love, joy, peace, forbearance, kindness, goodness, faithfulness, gentleness and self-control . . . let us keep in step with the Spirit.
>
> *Gal. 5:22–25*

In the same way as we learn from human parent figures, so we can learn from God, keeping in step with him, seeking to live the fruit of the Spirit.

But let's never forget that God's image is in our spiritual DNA.
He is in our nature as well as our nurture.
He put his image in us, and his image is like no other.
Becoming more like him as we grow spiritually older is a natural thing.
A nature thing.
And it's something we should desire.
Not so we can boast.
But so we can be real.
Be authentic.
Become like him.

Becoming like him is very becoming.

I see Jesus in you . . .

Look with my eyes. What do you see?

Becoming.

Father God, help me to see Jesus in others, and in me. Amen.

41

UNVEILED

Let us draw near to God with a sincere heart and with the full assurance that faith brings, having our hearts sprinkled to cleanse us from a guilty conscience . . .

Hebrews 10:22

Moses' face shone with the presence of God.[1] People were scared to go near him. Moses put a veil over his face, and they went near. But when it was just Moses and God, Moses took the veil away. Nothing in the way of God and him.

Paul wrote: '. . . a veil covers their hearts' (2 Cor. 3:15).

Unveiled, people didn't come near.
Perhaps the same can be true of our hearts. Or we feel it will be true.
We hide our true selves from others: our thoughts, our feelings, our insecurities.
If people truly knew us, if they saw us beyond 'Sunday Best' time, they might keep their distance. Better to keep the veil on.

Perhaps we feel God will keep his distance.
If he truly knew what we're like, he wouldn't come near.

> But whenever anyone turns to the Lord, the veil is taken away.
>
> *2 Cor. 3:16*

God is not people. He *does* know what we're like, and he *doesn't* keep his distance.

> My son, give me your heart and let your eyes delight in my ways . . .
>
> *Prov. 23:26*

Give me your heart.
Be yourself before me.
Unveil your heart.
Let nothing get in the way of us.
And let your eyes delight in my ways.
They're all around you.
See me not through the smokescreen of distance
but with unveiled eyes and heart.
Turn to me. When you do, the veil will be taken away.
Nothing between us.
Will you do it? Will you let your heart be unveiled to me?
It's safe. I promise I won't keep my distance . . .

Look with my eyes. What do you see?

Unveiled.

Father God, thank you that I am safe to be real with you. It may take me time, but I want to be. I know I am safe with you. Amen.

42

AMBASSADOR

We are therefore Christ's ambassadors, as though God were making his appeal through us. We implore you on Christ's behalf: be reconciled to God.

2 Corinthians 5:20

Ambassadors are often deployed to a foreign land. While there, they can't think, 'Oh actually, I'm going to have a day off from ambassadoring, and do the opposite of what my boss would want.' Everything about them represents and reflects the values of their boss.

The Israelites had been carried off to Babylon, an alien culture. Their captors mocked them: 'Sing songs of joy for us, sing about Zion', leading them to ask the question that has resonated through the centuries:

> How can we sing the songs of the LORD while in a foreign land?
>
> *Ps. 137:4*

As Christians, we are in a foreign land; heaven is our native home.
How can we sing the Lord's song?

The Israelites acknowledged they were in a place with different values from their own: a foreign land. Perhaps we, too, can gain – or regain – a longing for our native home.

They asked, 'How? How can we sing?' They were open to it being possible.

> Do [everything] as a representative of the Lord Jesus . . .
>
> *Col. 3:17, NLT*

We're his representatives. We have the privilege of representing him on earth.

> Christ has no body now but yours . . .
> Yours are the eyes with which he looks
> compassion on this world,
> Yours are the feet with which he walks to do good,
> Yours are the hands, with which he blesses all the world.
> Yours are the hands, yours are the feet,
> Yours are the eyes, you are his body.[1]

He's chosen us to be his ambassadors.
He's given us the score to sing from.
Are we open to it being possible?

Look with my eyes. What do you see?

Ambassador.

Father God, help me to sing your song, even when my words falter. It is an honour to be your ambassador. May I represent you well in everything. Amen.

SALT

You are the salt of the earth. But if the salt loses its saltiness, how can it be made salty again?

Matthew 5:13

Someone described as 'salt of the earth' is reliable, solid, dependable.
Did you know that calling someone 'salt of the earth' is echoing Jesus?
What about calling yourself 'salt of the earth'?
That's what Jesus says his disciples are.

In Old Testament times, salt was used in sacrifices to the Lord.[1]
Salt was a part of daily diet.
To 'eat salt with' someone meant to share their hospitality.

Just as salt was present in the meals and sacrifices in the Old Testament, just as salt is present in meals today, spiritual salt should be present in every aspect of our lives.
Salt is necessary.
It preserves, it heals, it flavours.
Salt makes things better.
Salt is you.
We are called to make things better, in Jesus' name.

How are you flavouring situations you encounter?
Do you make them better?
Do you bring Jesus in, remembering that you are his salt?

Something about salt; it is not responsible for getting itself to the food.
Someone else puts it there but, once it's there, it can do what it is meant to do.

Jesus is our Someone Else.

He decides where his salt goes, we don't have to do that, but wherever we find ourselves day-to-day, we are called to be salt.

To bring Jesus in.

To make things better.

Wherever he leads us, he wants us to bring him.

To encourage people to see him, meet him, get to know him.

To 'taste and see that the LORD is good' (Ps. 34:8).

Where will he sprinkle you from his saltshaker today?

Look with my eyes. What do you see?

Salt.

Father God, when you sprinkle your saltshaker today, let me willingly land where you choose. Help me make things better in your name. Amen.

44

PLUS ONE

God has said, 'Never will I leave you; never will I forsake you.'
Hebrews 13:5

'He's my Plus One.'
The words popped out of my mouth, summing up what I experienced but had never before articulated. I'd been asked how God helps me, and 'He's my Plus One' summed it up.

For me, being deaf can be hard. I might not feel confident walking into a social situation, because I can't hear. It can be quite isolating. Yet I'm not alone.
God is always with me.
My Plus One.
Reassuring.
Saying, 'We can do this together.'

Wedding invitations often include a Plus One. Invitees choose who they'd like to take with them.
Every situation in our lives includes a Plus One invitation.
Will we make it God?
Or will we make it worry, stress, busyness?
Those things may be present, but they don't have to be our chosen Plus One.

And what about God himself? The one who is 'over all and through all and in all' (Eph. 4:6).
Who's his Plus One? Who does he choose to have with him?
You.

> And what does the LORD require of you? To . . . walk humbly with your God.
>
> *Mic. 6:8*

Your name is God's Plus One. He wants you with him.
He knows what will happen tomorrow, and the next tomorrow.
He'll be there. And he puts your name on the invitation card.
Will you be my Plus One?
Will you be there with me?

He's your Plus One. You're his Plus One.
I don't know much about maths, but I do remember that two pluses make a positive.
Whatever we face, including the hard times – and there will be hard times – we have two pluses. Positively.

Look with my eyes. What do you see?

Plus One.

Father God, I choose a Plus One every day, and sometimes I forget to make it you. Please help me to choose you, not the other things. I know the other things will be easier to manage with you as my Plus One over all. Amen.

45 SPECIAL POSSESSION

But you are a chosen people, a royal priesthood, a holy nation, God's special possession . . .

1 Peter 2:9

Lost property at the school was full of jumpers.

The day had been unusually warm, the children discarding their jumpers as they played in the playground at lunchtime, forgetting them when they returned to afternoon class.

Rolling his eyes slightly, the site manager collected up the jumpers and deposited them in lost property. Sure enough, at the end of the school day, a trail of children arrived.

'Have you got my jumper?'

The jumpers all looked the same. Some were larger or smaller, but essentially, they looked the same. The site manager grabbed one, and held it out to the nearest child, 'Is this yours?' he asked hopefully.

The child shook her head, as did the next one. And the next.

The site manager thought he was going crazy, when his sanity was saved by a boy:

'Why don't you check the labels? Our names are on the labels.'

Soon, each jumper was restored to its rightful owner.

Including the very first jumper which, it turned out, did belong to the first child he'd asked.

Her name was on the label.

The girl didn't recognise her jumper, but she recognised her name.

Perhaps sometimes we don't recognise ourselves.

Circumstances overwhelm, busyness takes over, health deteriorates.

Is this you?

We shake our heads, expecting the label to read all the things we aren't.

Calm, sorted, successful, fun.

Not me.

Yet the label reads what we are. *Mine.*

God points to the label, and reads it:

You are

mine.[1]

My special possession.

This is you.

Look with my eyes. What do you see?

Special possession.

Father God, when I look at the label on my life, reading things on it that I'm not but think I am, help me to read it properly. I'm your special possession. That's who I am, regardless of anything else. Amen.

46 CHASED

The Lord is my shepherd, I lack nothing.

Psalm 23:1

At the start of lockdown 2020, unable to meet in person, people moved online.
Practise improved things and now, although we are not in lockdown, online meetings and events have become normal. They're convenient.

When I attend online events, I use live captions, which subtitle for me the things that people are saying.
I well remember the very first online event I attended, back in 2020.

It was a church service, and the reading was Psalm 23.
The reader read verse one: 'The Lord is my shepherd, I lack nothing.'
The captions read: 'The Lord is my shepherd, I *like* nothing.'

I sometimes wonder whether captions make Freudian slips.
They often make me think.
In this case, is it true?
Is it true that I like nothing?
Is it true that the Lord is my shepherd, and yet I am dissatisfied?

> The Lord is my shepherd . . .
> [His] goodness and love will follow me all the days of my life.
>
> *Ps. 23:6*

We're followed by his goodness and love.
Wherever we go, literally or metaphorically, his goodness and love follow us.
Not just follow, but chase.

God's goodness and love chase us.
They want to keep with us.
They don't want us getting away from knowing their presence.
Because God is our Shepherd.
And shepherds look after their sheep.

Look with my eyes. What do you see?

Chased.

Father God, is it true that I like nothing? I think it is, sometimes. Thank you that your goodness and love chase after me. Help me to notice them, and to truly know that in you, I lack nothing. Amen.

HABITED

Take my yoke upon you and learn from me, for I am gentle and humble in heart, and you will find rest for your souls.

Matthew 11:29

When Jesus says 'learn from me', the word he uses for 'learn' carries connotations of 'get into the habit of being'.[1]
Walk by my side and get into the habit of being taught by me.

I regularly, if not frequently, see nuns around and about.
They are often in hospitals, sometimes as patients but more often as visitors.
Bringing Jesus to bedsides, dressed in a habit.

Nuns are recognisable by their habits.
They are habited, which means dressed or clothed, from head to toe.

Walk by my side and get into the habit of being taught by me.
Clothed in the teachings of Jesus, from head to toe.

In Matthew 5, Jesus sat down to teach the people.
What was the first thing he taught?
What true blessing is:

> Blessed are the poor in spirit, for theirs is the kingdom of heaven.
> Blessed are those who mourn, for they will be comforted.
> Blessed are the meek, for they will inherit the earth.
> Blessed are those who hunger and thirst for righteousness, for they will be filled.
> Blessed are the merciful, for they will be shown mercy.
> Blessed are the pure in heart, for they will see God.
> Blessed are the peacemakers, for they will be called children of God.

> Blessed are those who are persecuted because of righteousness, for theirs is the kingdom of heaven.
>
> *Matt. 5:3–10*

Habited in the teachings of Jesus, we inhabit them.
Clothed in his teaching, from head to toe, we dwell in blessings, and we live them out.

Walk by my side and get into the habit of being taught by me.

Look with my eyes. What do you see?

Habited.

Father God, it's amazing to think that you want to help me learn, to teach me, to walk with me. I am very blessed. Help me to dwell in your blessings, to stay in them, to know them. To be consciously habited in them. Amen.

BREATH

We are the clay, you are the potter; we are all the work of your hand.

Isaiah 64:8

Dust on the ground.
Formed by God into a man.
I am the Potter, you are the clay.

Man in shape, in form, in look,
but not in life.
I am the Potter, you are the clay.

God breathes his breath into the man.
Life-less lives, becomes the breath of God.
I am the Potter, you are the clay.

Breath of God stands.
Stretches, lives, has children, children, children,
each carrying the breath of God.
I am the Potter, you are the clay.

Jesus.
God breathing the breath of God-in-Adam.
God-in-Adam breathes his last.

We breathe and we are breath.
Embodying the breath of God.
Breath is life, and 'in him we live and move and have our being' (Acts 17:28).

Carrying the breath of God.
Carrying life.
Carrying his life.
Alive because of him.
I am the Potter, you are the clay.

Look with my eyes. What do you see?

Breath.

Father God, help me remember to breathe. To stop and take deep breaths and, when I do, to know that I breathe and am breath. Your breath, living in me. I'm alive because of you and with you. May that encourage me, reassure me, affirm me. Amen.

49

COMPANY

And [they] heard the sound of the Lord God as he was walking in the garden in the cool of the day . . .

Genesis 3:8

'Can I come?' Children often ask this, and they are delighted when the answer is yes.
I think of children who have asked me, 'Will you come?' Their faces light up when I say yes.
What about my face? Do they stop to think that their excitement is mirrored in me?
Do they realise that their request for my company comes gift-wrapped?

As God's children, we can ask, 'Can I come?'
'Can I come and be part of what you're doing?'
And we can be delighted when the answer is **yes**.
When did you last ask God, *Can I come?*

A question reverberates around the garden.

> Where are you?
>
> *Gen. 3:9*

God asking where Adam and Eve are. He's missing their company.
Yes, he knows they've eaten the fruit he told them not to, and he knows that needs dealing with. He knows it has caused a rift. No, a chasm.
But at base level, he's missing their company.
He's missing spending time with them.
He's missing them. Is he missing you?
You're worth missing.

Adam and Eve deliberately avoided God's company.
Perhaps you are doing the same.
Or perhaps you're not deliberately avoiding his company, more it's just kind of happened.
He's arrived at points where you'd usually check in, and ended up looking around, asking 'Where are you?'
Maybe it's difficult to answer that question. You're not sure where you are.
I'm grumpy. I'm scared. I'm worried. I'm stressed. I'm anxious. But I don't know how to say it.
What about showing him instead, by answering yes to his, **Can I come?**

Can I come?
Yes.
Where are you? Let me show you . . .

Look with my eyes. What do you see?

Company.

Father God, when I have no words, and I don't know where I am, help me to let you come into those places with me. Help me show them to you and know that, even in the mess, you want my company. Amen.

50

HANDS-FULL

With weapons of righteousness in the right hand and in the left . . .
2 Corinthians 6:7

Moses is not sure. God is asking him to go to the Israelite elders, and tell them that God is going to rescue them from slavery. It's not that Moses doesn't believe God, but he can't believe that the elders will listen to him. 'What if they don't believe me, or listen to me, and think I'm making it up?'[1]
God replies with a question of his own: **'What's that in your hand?'[2]**

Moses blinks in surprise. He's just told God what he's worried about, and he's pretty sure he didn't mention his hands. Wasn't God listening?
He looks down. 'I have a staff in my hand.'
God's question points to an answer.
God was certainly listening.

In the Bible, a staff represented leadership.
What was in Moses' hand answered Moses' question.
What if they don't believe me? **Look in your hand.**

Moses was very human. Don't we all have 'what if' times?
What if things go wrong/I can't do it/I look stupid . . .
What's that in your hand?
. . . weapons of righteousness in the right hand and in the left . . .

Check your hands.
I have weapons of righteousness in my hand.
Righteousness here means 'the act of doing what is in agreement with God's standards'[3] and 'The state of being in a proper relationship with God'.

When we face doubts, and doubters, from outside and inside, let's look in our hands.
We have weapons to fight those doubts.
Weapons to help us align with God's standards rather than our own.
Weapons to help us look at ourselves with his eyes.
Weapons of righteousness.

Look with my eyes. What do you see?

Hands-full.

Father God, thank you that you are always listening. Help me to remember that, even when things don't make sense. I want to hold on tight to my weapons of righteousness, batting away doubt and welcoming truth. Help me to check my hands. Amen.

51

TEAMED

Suppose one of you has a hundred sheep and loses one of them. Doesn't he leave the ninety-nine in the open country and go after the lost sheep until he finds it?

Luke 15:4

We decided to play a game, moving chairs around so that everyone would have a seat.
'Will you be on my team?' one of the children asked me.
The same child who'd just said, giggling, 'Aunty Memem is not good at this game!'
'Wouldn't you rather go with someone else?' I asked.
Shaking his head, he led me to two chairs side-by-side.

We didn't win. But in a way, we did. We had fun, we enjoyed being on the same team, we looked at the instructions, we discussed what to do. We were together.
For my nephew, choosing his team was about the person, not the skills.

At school, team captains often choose their friends first, regardless of how good their friends are at netball. Someone is always left till last, reluctantly tolerated by the captain of the team they join.

In Luke 15, Jesus told a story about a sheep that went missing from the flock.
The shepherd searched and searched, and brought the sheep home.
The sheep wasn't reluctantly tolerated by the shepherd.
The sheep was found, celebrated and brought back into the fold, despite running off in the first place.

Jesus is the Shepherd, and you are the sheep.
Whatever you do, however far you stray, Jesus wants to bring you home.
He searches for you.

Will you be on my team?
But I'm not very good; choose someone else.
He shakes his head, and takes your hand . . .
I choose you.
You nod, and don't pull away.

Jesus searches for you and, wherever you are, he'll find you.

Look with my eyes. What do you see?

Teamed.

Father God, I'm used to being left till last. I'm used to leaving myself till last. Thank you that you bring me back from there, finding me, choosing me, wanting me on your team. Amen.

COVERED

He will cover you with his feathers, and under his wings you will find refuge . . .

Psalm 91:4

'Cover' in Psalm 91 means to spread protection, as does wings.
A refuge is a place of safety, protection, shelter.
Somewhere to receive help when things are tough.

He will spread protection over you, and under the protective reach of his power you shall find refuge.

'I've got you covered' is a phrase people use to mean: *Leave it to me, you can rely on me.*

Did you know God says, **I've got you covered**?
Whatever situation, wherever you go;
I've got you covered.
You can rely on me.

When panic sets in.
You're under my protective reach.
I've got you covered.

When to-do lists are overwhelming.
You're under my protective reach.
I've got you covered.

When it's hard to breathe.
You're under my protective reach.
I've got you covered.

When you're in pain.
You're under my protective reach.
I've got you covered.

You can rely on me.
My banner over you is love.[1]

Look with my eyes. What do you see?

Covered.

Father God, thank you for your protection covering me, wherever I go and whatever I feel. Help me learn what it means to take refuge in and under your protective reach. Amen.

SAFE

Then the LORD said, 'There is a place near me where you may stand on a rock.'

Exodus 33:21

'Show me your glory.'
The words were out. Was I being cheeky? Was I asking too much?
I need it, though. I need to see and be reminded of who he is.

'I will cause all my goodness to pass in front of you' (v. 19).
It's happening.
'I will proclaim my name, the LORD, in your presence' (v. 19).
But you can't see my face.
He sees my disappointment.
No one may see my face and live.
He wants me to live? I'm not sure I want to live.
At least, not my life. What about . . .
His words break through:

There is a place near me, a place that's for you.
I do want you to live.
There is a place near me, a place that's for you.
Stand there, and look out for my goodness
There is a place near me, a place that's for you.
You'll see my goodness from there,
every way you look.
There's a place near me, a place that's for you,
near me.
When my glory passes by . . .
His glory? His face? But if I see them, I won't live.
And this place near him makes life better.

. . . **'I will put you in a cleft in the rock and cover you with my hand'** (v. 22).
Why?
He answers my unspoken thought:

Because I want you safe.
There's a place near me
A place that's for you . . .

> You are my hiding-place; you will protect me . . .
>
> *Ps. 32:7*

Look with my eyes. What do you see?

Safe.

Father God, help me to live in your presence. Please put me in the cleft in the rock, where I am safe. Amen.

54

FRIEND

There is a friend who sticks closer than a brother.
Proverbs 18:24

I read an article about loneliness.
Isolation is increasing.
Friends are few.

In John 15:15, Jesus tells his disciples, 'I have called you friends.'
Jesus calls us friends.
Verse 16 says that he chose us to be his friends.
Jesus looked around the world and chose you as his friend.

I was co-leading a retreat. One evening in the dining room, the little girl who was there came over, something held tight in her little hand. 'I got this for you.'
It was a stone.
I thanked her, and she smiled at me before heading back to her table to tuck into dessert.

Later, I looked at the stone. I felt it's shape. Beyond the window were millions of stones, making up the beach. Why had she chosen this particular stone for me?
As I looked, I realised it didn't matter. I could spend ages trying to figure it out, or I could simply enjoy the fact that she had. I didn't need to know why.

Maybe we wonder why Jesus chose us to be his friends.
But we don't need to know why. We can simply enjoy the fact that he did.

The disciples would soon betray Jesus.
Jesus knew that.
And he deliberately called them friends.
We may sometimes not follow Jesus as we'd like to.
Jesus knows that.
And he deliberately calls us friends.

A friend is a person you know well, and like.
Jesus knows you well.
And he likes you a lot.
You're his friend.

Look with my eyes. What do you see?

Friend.

Father God, how incredible that you chose me to be your friend! I like being your friend. Amen.

SEEN

She [Hagar] gave this name to the LORD who spoke to her: 'You are the God who sees me,' for she said, 'I have now seen the One who sees me.'

Genesis 16:13

I am seen.
In the wilderness of life,
beside streams of provision
or far from them,
I am seen.
I forget that I'm seen.

By the stream,
I have what I need
but things don't feel so good.
And I long to be noticed (really noticed – by someone – anyone),
I forget that I'm seen.

Far from the stream,
I don't have what I need.
Trouble looms.
I'm all alone, I want it to end.
I forget that I'm seen.

Seen by the One who sees everything.
The One who sees through.
Sees through the smile to my despair.
Sees through to the silent screams behind my coping.
Who knows me inside out,
yet never looks away.

I am seen.

Being seen, I dare return his gaze.
And I live in his seeing.

By the stream.
In the wilderness.
I live seen.[1]

Look with my eyes. What do you see?

Seen.

Father God, sometimes I feel invisible. No one sees me. I lose sight of myself. Thank you that you see me. Give me courage to believe that you never look away. Amen.

56

HOME

'Return to me, and I will return to you,' says the LORD Almighty.
Malachi 3:7

He's running. Sprinting. So embarrassing.
Holding his robes up. I see his bare legs! Shameful.
As if the family haven't had enough shame as it is, what with the youngest son taking his fortune, going off to the Gentiles, and wasting all his money. Well, if that boy comes home with his tail between his legs, I'll organise the Kezazah ceremony myself. I'll break a pot in front of him and shout that he's now cut off from his people.

I see them staring, but I don't care. I only wish I could run faster. I've got to get to my boy before they do. I saw him coming; I've been watching for him ever since he left.
I hear them muttering Kezazah. He's not getting cut off. Not on my watch.

I'm so ashamed.
If I could turn back the clock, I would.
I'd never have left home.
I should have stayed with Dad.
I've got nothing now.
I don't even know if I should go home, but home is the only place I can go.
Who's that? Running?
It looks like Dad. But Dad wouldn't run.
It is Dad. My dad is running.
Maybe he doesn't know the village is following.
Such shame. I'd better hide.
If he comes near me, if he's seen near me, it'll make things worse.

It's too late.
Dad's hugging me.
I'm hugging him back.
Welcome home, son.

'Shame on you.'
They're talking to my dad . . .[1]

Look with my eyes. What do you see?

Home.

Father God, thank you that you always watch for me, and welcome me home. Home is where you are. May I always be home. Amen.

ACCOMPANIED

When you go through deep waters, I will be with you. When you go through rivers of difficulty, you will not drown.

Isaiah 43:2a, NLT

'Where is he?'

Joseph broke off his conversation, looking around, hoping to be able to answer Mary's question. 'He'll be here somewhere.'

But there was no sign of Jesus.

'Where is he?'

Frantic now, they searched.

They asked travelling companions.

There were lots of people on the road heading away from Jerusalem, but none had seen Jesus. 'I thought he was on this road, too.'

Mary choked back sobs.

They realised that they'd last seen Jesus in Jerusalem.

Together, they turned round, walking against the flow of people.

They found him in the temple.

Didn't you know I'd be in my Father's house?

Didn't you know I'd be where God is?[1]

Where is God?

God is with you.

One day it was a puddle, and now it's an ocean. **I know.**

I thought I could handle it. **I know.**

I'm walking through difficult waters. **I know.**

I feel as though the waves will overwhelm me. **I know.**

One day it was a puddle, and now it's an ocean. **I know.**

I should be able to handle it. **No, my child. Don't put that burden on yourself.**

But people think I – **I know.**
How do you know? **Because I'm in it with you.**
You're with me in the ocean? **I am.**
We can handle it. **We can.**
I'm walking through difficult waters. ***We* are walking through difficult waters.**
The waves are overwhelming me. **I won't let you drown.**

Look with my eyes. What do you see?

Accompanied.

Father God, sometimes I can be like Mary and Joseph, travelling on, assuming you are going in the same direction. Help me to accompany you through life, as you accompany me, so that we will be going in the same direction. Amen.

58

SENT

Jesus said, 'Peace be with you! As the Father has sent me, I am sending you.'

John 20:21

The man had been born blind.
He didn't know what seeing was.
He couldn't see Jesus, maybe didn't even know Jesus was there.
But Jesus saw him, exactly where he was.
The man didn't need to change to be seen.
Jesus moved to be with him, not the other way round.

What about you? Do you know that Jesus is walking with you?

Perhaps, when we struggle to see Jesus, staying still is good.
He's promised he will come to us.

> I will not leave you as orphans; I will come to you.
>
> *John 14:18*

Jesus puts some mud on the man's eyes, and tells him to go and 'wash in the Pool of Siloam' (John 9:7). The man washed, and his sight was restored. Siloam means 'sent'. The man washed in 'sent', and was sent into his life.

It can be easy to think of 'being sent by God' as only something for missionaries, or evangelists, or pastors.
It is for them.
It's for the rest of us, too.
Those of us who are parents, who are cleaners, who are teachers, who are housebound, who are accountants, who are neighbours . . .
It's for all of us.
God knows what our days will hold, and he sends us into them.

Each morning, as I clean my teeth, I do physiotherapy stretches.
I fit them into my normal routine.
What about fitting 'washing in sent' into our morning routines?
As we wash our faces, we could remind ourselves that God is sending us into today.
And he begins his sending with peace . . .
Peace be with you today.

Look with my eyes. What do you see?

Sent.

Father God, thank you for seeing me where I am. Even when I struggle to see you in my life, you are there. Sending me into my days. Sending me with your peace. Please help me carry your peace with me, whatever else happens. Amen.

59

EMPOWERED

'Not by might nor by power, but by my Spirit,' says the LORD Almighty.

Zechariah 4:6

What's that noise? It sounds like wind coming from heaven.
What's that over his head? It looks like fire.
It's on everyone's head, including mine.

We rushed out of the house, and whenever we spoke, everyone could understand.
Jerusalem is full of people of all languages at the moment, and they all knew what we were saying. It was amazing. People thought we were drunk, but Peter told everyone it was the Holy Spirit come on us.[1]

The Holy Spirit enabling us.
The Holy Spirit is amazing.
God gave him to us.

> The Spirit helps us in our weakness. We do not know what we ought to pray for, but the Spirit himself intercedes for us through wordless groans.
>
> *Rom. 8:26*

Maybe you don't know what to pray. *Come, Holy Spirit.*
Maybe you don't know what to do. *Come, Holy Spirit.*
Maybe you don't know what to say. *Come, Holy Spirit.*
Maybe you don't know how to bring peace. *Come, Holy Spirit.*
Maybe . . . *Come, Holy Spirit.*

'The Spirit helps us in our weakness.'

What's that noise? Listen for it.
What's over your head? Look for it.

The Holy Spirit.
The power of God.
Listen.
Look.
Trust.

Look with my eyes. What do you see?

Empowered.

Father God, thank you for empowering me. Come, Holy Spirit. Amen.

60 BEAUTIFUL

I am weathered but still elegant . . .

Song of Songs 1:5, MSG

'I am weathered'.
Weathered skin was considered undesirable at the time, particularly by well-to-do women.
'I am weathered'.
This woman had a difficult life, a tough background, family conflicts.
'I am weathered'.
The woman had worked for her family, in the fields, under the sun.
She was weathered because of her background.
Her brothers forced her to look after vineyards, and looking after herself no longer happened.

Do you have a 'weathered'? Things you would notice about yourself in a non-complimentary way?

During one of my brain surgeries, my facial nerve was damaged. I had a half-smile. I didn't like it. My facial nerve is still damaged. I still have a wonky smile. I still don't like it.
But let me tell you what made it easier.
A friend, after seeing a photo of me back before the damage, saying, 'I prefer you now, because that's how I know you.'
The damage – the 'weathered' – didn't disappear, but despite it she preferred me now.

> I am dark but beautiful . . .
>
> *Song 1:5*, NLT

The woman learned that sun damage didn't stop her being beautiful. Not to the one who mattered. She learned, as I have learned, that we are more than we see in the mirror.

God looks at us, in all our weaknesses and troubles and struggles, and names us 'chosen' and 'special' (1 Pet. 2:9).

The woman in Song of Songs is called 'Beloved'.

The man is called 'Lover'.[1]

She's beloved because of him, and so she dares believe that although she is weathered, she is beautiful.

Damage doesn't stop us being beautiful.

Not to the one who matters.

Look with my eyes. What do you see?

Beautiful.

Father God, I am weathered. Weathered from so much. Help me to add 'but beautiful' and believe that to you, the One who matters, I am beloved. Weathered does not stop me being beautiful to you. Amen.

61

WELCOME

So now there is no condemnation for those who belong to Christ Jesus.

***Romans 8:1*, NLT**

Philemon paced back and forth, the letter in his hand.
He read and re-read it, but the words never changed.
Paul really was asking him to take Onesimus back.
No, more than that.
Philemon glanced at the letter again.
Yes, *welcome him back as a brother, not as a slave.*

Philemon shook his head. Was Paul being serious?
Welcome as a brother a slave who stole and ran away?
A slave whose punishment should be death?

Philemon paced, remembering his first meeting with Paul.
Paul's preaching had meant so much to him, it had led him to Christ.
Paul never wasted words or said anything he didn't mean.
And now Paul's words – written from prison, of all places – were asking him to do the unthinkable.

'Jesus, what should I do?' Philemon was growing used to praying.
Jesus. The One who'd given his life for Philemon.
The One from whom Philemon had received a new life.
Paul said Jesus did that willingly.[1]
He wanted to do it, so he could welcome Philemon into a new life with him.

Philemon smiled. His new life with Jesus was better than he'd ever known.
What was it about the letter that rattled him so?
He knew the answer: Onesimus didn't deserve to be welcomed back.
And you did? Philemon was growing used to hearing Jesus in his heart, too.

He discarded the letter. Message received and understood.
His own welcome had depended on Jesus, not on him.
Onesimus's welcome depended on Philemon, not on Onesimus.
'Καλώς ήρθες, αδερφέ'
'Welcome, brother.'

> Christ has welcomed you . . .
>
> *Rom. 15:7,* ESV

Look with my eyes. What do you see?

Welcome.

Father God, thank you for welcoming me. Help me to welcome others as you welcome me; unreservedly and without point-scoring. Amen.

62

APPLE

Keep me as the apple of your eye . . .

Psalm 17:8a

The phrase 'the apple of my eye', meaning someone valuable and precious, was first used in the Bible. The Hebrew literally means 'little man of the eye', because of the tiny little reflection of yourself that you can see in another person's pupils, if you are close enough.

In Psalm 17, when David asks God to 'Keep me as the little man of your eye', he's asking God to focus on him and watch him closely.
Guard me, watch me so closely that my image is central in your eyes.

Keep me as the apple of your eye . . .

I like being the apple of your eye.
I like you watching over me so closely.
I like my reflection being in your eyes.
I like being precious to you.
I like being the little person of your eye.
But what about when I mess up?
You're the little person of my eye, I never look away.
Even when I'm grumpy?
You're the little person of my eye even then.
When I'm anxious? **Then, too.**
When I'm sleeping? **Yes.**
When I'm busy? **You're the little person of my eye, always.**
I'm central in your eyes? **You are.**
So everything I do, I do in your eyes?
Yes. I'm always focused on you.
Nothing matters more than you.

You're the little person of my eye.
I see you when you dance.
I see you when you cry.
Your life happens in my eyes.

> The LORD will watch over your coming and going both now and for evermore.
>
> *Ps. 121:8*

Look with my eyes. What do you see?

Apple.

Father God, I never thought I'd be glad to be an apple, but I am. Thank you for making me the little person of your eye, watching over me so closely. Amen.

63

COMFORTED

Jesus wept.

John 11:35

'I hate this.'
That day, I'd been told I needed more surgery.
Now, curled up in bed, all I could hurl at God was, 'I hate this.'
Even as I said it, part of me recoiled.
Was it OK to say that to God?
I didn't know.
I began to cry, and God cried with me.
I hate it, too.

In John 11, one of Jesus' closest friends – Lazarus – has died.
Before Jesus arrives at Lazarus's grave, he is met outside the village by Lazarus's sisters.
When he sees Mary crying, he is moved.
He cares deeply.
Her pain is his pain.
Our pain is his.

Jesus talked with the sisters. **Where have you laid Lazarus?**
Come and see.
At the invitation to come and see, Jesus wept.
Then the Jews said, 'See how he loved him!' (John 11:36).
Jesus' tears were recognised as a sign of his love.

Have you invited him to love you with tears?
When we invite Jesus to 'come and see' our empty, broken, dead, 'I hate this' places, and allow him to cry with us, we know his love-in-tears; a precious thing to know.

As I lay in bed, crying, God didn't say, *It's OK, I'll heal you.*
He didn't say, *Will you stop crying?*
I hate it, too.
Come and see.

God saw and he stayed.
He shared.
He loved.
Love-in-tears.

Look with my eyes. What do you see?

Comforted.

Father God, sometimes I hide my tears. I never need to hide them from you. Help me open my heart to your love-in-tears, and to go deeper with you. Amen.

64

CLEAN

Create in me a pure heart, O God, and renew a steadfast spirit within me.

Psalm 51:10

Not long ago, Jesus and his disciples shared a meal at a home in Bethany, and a woman anointed Jesus.
It wasn't the first time something like that had happened.
And Jesus had called it 'a beautiful thing'.

Now, during a more private meal, Jesus stands and picks up a towel and a bowl of water.
What he's about to do is unusual.
The job of a servant.

Jesus makes his way around the group, washing their feet.
Why?
To show them 'the full extent of his love' (John 13:1, NIV 1984).

Jesus reaches Peter.
Peter jerks back,
recoiling,
pulling his feet out of sight.
Jesus stands there, holding the towel and bowl.

If I don't, Peter, there will be something in the way of you and me.

Peter stills.
Raises his eyes to Jesus.
Takes a deep breath.
'Then wash me.'

Here are my dirty feet.
You can see them, Jesus.
I might flinch, but I won't run.
My dirt won't take me from you.
Jesus kneels.
Sees dirt.
Gently cradles a dusty foot in his hands,
showing Peter how much he loves him.
You're doing a beautiful thing.

Look with my eyes. What do you see?

Clean.

Father God, give me courage to let you see and wash my dirty feet. Help me not to run, but to stay. To be wiped clean. To hear you whisper, 'You're doing a beautiful thing.' Amen.

65 CLOSE

Know that the LORD is God. It is he who made us, and we are his; we are his people, the sheep of his pasture.

Psalm 100:3

Peter, James and John.
The privileged three.
They were especially close to Jesus.
They were the ones chosen to go up the mountain.[1]
Climbing higher and higher with Jesus.
Invited to share in that special moment when Jesus was transfigured,
his face shining,
himself wrapped in light.
Invited to hear the voice, God's voice:
'This is my Son. I love him. I'm pleased with him.'

Peter, James and John.
The privileged three.
They were especially close to Jesus.
They were the ones chosen to go deeper in the garden.[2]
Invited to hear Jesus say his soul was hurting.
He was troubled.
Invited to hear him pray.
Invited to hear absence.
No voice of God speaking this time.

Peter, James and John.
The privileged three.
They were especially close to Jesus.
They were invited to share with him.
To know his heart.

A heart that beat with joy.
A heart that beat with grief.

> He gathers the lambs in his arms and carries them close to his heart . . .
>
> *Isa. 40:11*

You're invited to catch his heartbeat, too.
What a privilege.

Look with my eyes. What do you see?

Close.

Father God, hold me close. Let me catch your heartbeat. Amen.

66

HIGHLIGHTED

But a poor widow came and put in two very small copper coins, worth only a few pence.

Mark 12:42

My niece showed me her new highlighter pens, ready to highlight words on a page that she felt were extra important. Words that might otherwise get lost in the body of text.

The widow had someone in her life, and now he was gone.
In Jesus' day, widows were treated badly. They were looked down on, and disregarded. That's not how it was meant to be. Back in Deuteronomy, God made special provision for widows, saying they must be looked after, not looked down on.
Why did God need to make this a law? Presumably because people were mistreating widows. And God said **don't do it**. And God said **be kind to widows**.

Perhaps something in your life has changed. A situation you wouldn't have chosen, or perhaps daily things are taken from you: confidence, self-esteem. You feel, in a sense, widowed. You have nothing left to give.
Perhaps you are mistreated. That's not what God wants.

> He defends the cause of the . . . widow . . .
>
> *Deut. 10:18*

He says **don't do it**.

Jesus was watching people in the temple.
Lots of rich people ostentatiously threw money into the temple offering. '*Look at me.*'

The widow quietly put in two small coins. '*Don't look at me.*'
Jesus saw them all.
They all gave.
And Jesus highlighted the widow.

> She, out of her poverty, put in everything . . .
>
> *Mark 12:44*

Are you impoverished? Feeling insignificant? Spiritually, emotionally, physically?
Give it to Jesus. What you give matters. And if you give from a widow place, know that Jesus values you and what you give. He highlights you. He cares.
Jesus notices the widows . . .

Look with my eyes. What do you see?

Highlighted.

Father God, when I lose myself in the crowds, help me remember that you highlight me. You notice me. I do give from a widow place; let me give anyway, knowing that you understand true value. Amen.

NEW

See, I am doing a new thing! Now it springs up; do you not perceive it? I am making a way in the wilderness and streams in the wasteland.

Isaiah 43:19

They're gone! Jesus got rid of the demons for me.
He basically told them to get lost, and they did!
Now people don't talk about me as Mary who has seven demons, they say Mary who *had* seven demons.[1]
I think of myself in the same way.
As I follow Jesus, I'm so aware of what I was before I met him.
People avoided me, scared of me. I hated my life.
Then Jesus came.
How can we all not refer to me as Mary who *had* seven demons.

I've been following Jesus for a while now. I can't get enough time with him.
People still call me Mary who had seven demons.
I'm beginning to wish they wouldn't. More and more, I'm simply thinking of myself as Mary, though 'who had seven demons' often slips in.
I feel caught between who I was and who I am.

I have bigger things to worry about. Jesus, my Jesus, is hanging on a cross.
He's dying. He's dead. I don't care what they call me now. Nothing matters.

They buried him in a tomb, and put a stone in front.
I'm going there tomorrow. I need to be where he is.

The stone has been pushed aside.
Jesus' body is not there.
I don't know where they've put him.

'Mary.' I instinctively wait for the rest. '*Who had seven demons.*'
But the label doesn't come.
And I recognise the voice it doesn't come from.
Jesus.

> Therefore, if anyone is in Christ, the new creation has come: the old has gone, the new is here!
>
> *2 Cor. 5:17*

Look with my eyes. What do you see?

New.

Father God, who I was does pull me back. The me before I met you is still there. Help me come to you to be made new, again and again. Amen.

68

BĀNÂ

I will build you up again, and you, Virgin Israel, will be rebuilt. Again you will take up your tambourines and go out to dance with the joyful.

Jeremiah 31:4

'Who chooses the music?' I asked my anaesthetist, before surgery.
'Not me!' he said, with a smile, 'but I don't pay attention to the music. I'm too busy checking on you.'
He anaesthetised me, and I was anaesthetised.
All I needed to do was allow myself to be so.

Israel had strayed from God.
They'd turned away. They'd looked elsewhere. They'd wanted to be like everyone else.
And, bit by bit, they'd crumbled.
They'd been captured, carried off, and their country taken from them.
They were rubble. They were ruins.
And God told them to get a grip and pull themselves together.

No, he didn't.
He said, **I'll do it. I'll build you up. All you need to do is allow yourself to be rebuilt**.

The words translated 'build' and 'rebuilt' are the same word in Hebrew: bānâ. Build and rebuilt are one, build being active and rebuilt being passive.

Maybe we feel as though we are crumbling.
Life is stressful. We're juggling many plates.
We have a worrying health diagnosis. We're worried about finances.
We've lost our joy in the Lord. We've looked elsewhere.
We've crumbled.

And God whispers, **I will 'bānâ' – that's my job; and you will *be* 'bānâ' – that's your job.**

If we want to be rebuilt, restored, shaped into who God has in mind, we need to let go.
Hand it over to him. Be.
Be one with him. Be.
Not looking elsewhere. Be.
Be bānâ.
And hold onto the promise:
Again you will dance . . .

Look with my eyes. What do you see?

Bānâ.

Father God, when you and I have done our 'bānâ' jobs, please help me dance again. Amen.

KIND

Six of the towns you give the Levites will be cities of refuge, to which a person who has killed someone may flee.

Numbers 35:6

In the year ending March 2023, there were 590 homicides recorded in the UK.[1]
The vast majority of people are not murderers.
We do not kill. Or do we?
To kill is to cause the end of a living thing.

We have the Spirit living in us, see Galatians 5.
Love, joy, peace, patience, kindness, goodness, faithfulness, gentleness, self-control.[2]
Do we sometimes cause an end to those things, in ourselves and other people?

Have I killed someone's joy today?
Have I killed my kindness today?
Have I killed someone's faith today?

If homicides were measured by this, how many would happen daily?
They do happen.
Where can we go when they do?

> Lead me to the rock that is higher than I.
>
> *Ps. 61:2*

We can go to our refuge. Our safe place. Jesus.
He is our city of refuge.

Rahab lived in the walls of the city of Jericho.
She wasn't perfect. Yet, when the city was destroyed, it was she who hung a scarlet cord from her window.[3]
A sign that kept her safe. A sign that symbolises the blood of Jesus.

Galatians 5 homicides will happen. And when they do, we have a refuge.
A safe place.
Our place is Jesus. Let's go there. Let's not kill kindness towards ourselves.

You have a refuge. Everywhere you go, everything you do, every situation you face, I'm sheltering you. Don't kill your kindness. Run to me. I'm waiting to protect you from life's batterings. You have a refuge. Me.[4]

Look with my eyes. What do you see?

Kind.

Father God, I don't do well at being kind to myself. Help me to learn from you, and to be kind enough to myself to turn to you. Amen.

VALUED

So don't be afraid; you are worth more than many sparrows.
Matthew 10:31

Psalm 84 was probably written during the time of the exile.
The temple would have been in ruins, and what do we read in verse 3?
'Even the sparrow has found a home . . . a place near your altar'.
The sparrow flew in among the ruins and settled near God's altar.

Jesus knew his disciples would face opposition.
They'd be betrayed, arrested, persecuted.
Jesus didn't pretend otherwise, but he did say:
'Don't be afraid. You're worth more than many sparrows.'

Perhaps the disciples recalled a Scripture:
Even the sparrow has found a home near your altar.
Perhaps they remembered that the home was among ruins.
Backs straightened, shoulders back, heads up.
They were worth more than sparrows.
They hadn't realised they were so valued.
Knowing their worth would help them with the task ahead.

The sparrow who found a place near the altar would one day be sacrificed at the altar.[1]
As we follow Jesus, we will be called to make sacrifices.
The Psalm 84 sparrow was in the temple, by the altar, a special place to be, and the temple was in ruins.
The sparrow offered as a sacrifice was in a restored temple, a beautiful building.

As we grow in Jesus, as we are called to make – and be – sacrifices, the places where we go are made beautiful by his presence with us.

Do you know how much Jesus values you?
Has your heart heard him encourage you to know?

Don't be afraid; you're worth more than many sparrows.

May his affirmation equip and encourage you today, and tomorrow, and tomorrow . . .

Look with my eyes. What do you see?

Valued.

Father God, give me the ability to grasp your valuing of me, and may it strengthen me in the days to come. Amen.

RESTER

Take my yoke upon you and learn from me, for I am gentle and humble in heart, and you will find rest for your souls.

Matthew 11:29

In the Old Testament, being yoked was oppressive.
In Leviticus 26:13, God declares that he led the Israelites from slavery in Egypt; he broke the yoke that bound them to Egypt and 'enabled you to walk with heads held high'.
Isaiah 10, the Israelites are again oppressed, this time by the Assyrians, and God again promises to break that yoke.

To be yoked is to be attached to, taken in the same direction as.
What might we be yoked to today?
Money? Status? Job? Health?
What about Jesus? Are we yoked to him?
Those who heard his words 'take my yoke upon you' would have known about yokes.
They'd have known the history of being forcibly yoked.
Yokes were not good, yet Jesus makes being yoked seem a positive thing.

Take my yoke upon you . . .
They had a choice. No one was forcing them.
Learn from me . . .
Get into the habit of being taught by me.
Someone wanted to teach them, not beat them?
I am gentle and humble . . .
They were allowed to be yoked to gentle? To humble?
You will find rest for your souls . . .
The word Jesus uses for 'rest' means 'a resting place'.[1]
Yoked to Jesus is a resting place;

a place where we don't need to have all the answers.
Learn from me.
Get into the habit of resting in my knowing.
A place where we are allowed to be treated gently.

Whatever happens in life, however hard things get, we are yoked to a Resting Place.
Or we can be.
We can learn to be.
Take my yoke upon you . . .

Look with my eyes. What do you see?

Rester.

Father God, I have a resting place. Wherever I go, whatever I do, however busy and stressed I get, I have a resting place. I'm yoked to it. Help me to always 'take your yoke upon me' so I live in a resting place. Amen.

ROYAL

For God is the King of all the earth . . .

Psalm 47:7a

Shakespeare's *Love's Labour's Lost* is centred around a young princess who suddenly finds herself catapulted into being queen when her father dies.
I saw the play and, when the princess appeared in her regal robes at the end, she looked so young. She seemed more child-like than she had before.

The Bible tells us that when we become Christians, we are made royal by becoming children. Children of the King.
Children of God, with Jesus, the Son of God, as our brother.[1]
When we believe in Jesus, and his cross, and resurrection, we are catapulted into royalty.

Jesus said:

> Truly I tell you, unless you change and become like little children, you will never enter the kingdom of heaven. Therefore, whoever takes the lowly position of this child is the greatest in the kingdom of heaven.
>
> *Matt. 18:3–4*

The new queen appeared child-like and, emulating her father, was the most important person in the land.
When we become like little children, relying on and emulating our Father and our Big Brother, we become great.
Perhaps not in the kingdom of this world, but in the kingdom of heaven.
In God's kingdom.
We are related to the King of kings.

When we wear the royal robes God gives us, we mark ourselves out as his. We stay close: he doesn't send our clothes in the mail, they are hand-given.

The Greek word Jesus used for 'greatest' carries a connotation of 'more'.
Wearing our royal robes, we become more.
More like him.
More child-like.
More fitted for, and fitting into, the kingdom of heaven.

Look with my eyes. What do you see?

Royal.

Father God, thank you for my royal robes. When I wear them, may they remind me I'm your child. When I live my adult life and responsibilities, I can turn to you, and share things with you and, as I do, I will become more . . . Amen.

73

GOD'S JOY

Nehemiah said, 'Go and enjoy choice food and sweet drinks, and send some to those who have nothing prepared . . . Do not grieve, for the joy of the LORD is your strength.'

Nehemiah 8:10

It's an interesting phrase, 'joy of the Lord'.
I've generally taken it to mean us finding joy in him, in the joy he gives us; which I think it does mean. But perhaps the 'of' is a sort of homonym; a word that has different meanings. Maybe it is not only talking about our joy here, but God's joy, too.
Could it also mean that we can find strength by knowing that God finds joy in us?
That we make him glad?

> The LORD your God is with you . . . He will take great delight in you . . . he will . . . rejoice over you . . .
>
> *Zeph. 3:17*

When we feel insufficient, incapable, unconfident, perhaps we can find within a voice that refuses to be silenced: I am God's joy.
When we can do nothing: *I am God's joy.*
When our strength is lacking: *I am God's joy.*
When we have 'nothing prepared': *I am God's joy.*

The words in Nehemiah specify those who have nothing prepared, who don't feel ready, who are not in the 'joy zone'.
I am God's joy.
Try it.
Because it's true.
You are God's joy.
Including at times when you are not your own joy.

When surgeries take abilities from me, or I'm lacking in confidence, or all I see in me is damage, I am certainly not my own joy. In those times, I have learned to whisper from the rubbish: *I am God's joy*, and to hear and believe his response: **Yes, you are.**

Yes, you are gives me strength.

To know his peace, to face the day.

I am God's joy.

What do you see? Look with my eyes.

God's joy.

Father God. I am your joy? Me? Help me to believe your **Yes, you are**. When I live my days and situations as your joy, I think it will help. Who has to deal with x/y/z I'm facing? God's joy. That's me. Amen.

MET

My soul thirsts for God, for the living God. When can I go and meet with God?

Psalm 42:2

'Simon, do you love me?' asks Jesus.
You remember that Simon Peter had denied all knowledge of Jesus, so Jesus' question seems fair. **Do you love me?**
'Yes,' says Simon, 'You know I'm fond of you.'
Fond? But that's not what Jesus asked. He must have spotted the difference, too, because he asks again,
'Simon, do you truly love me?'
'Yes,' says Simon. 'You know I'm fond of you.'
But that's not what Jesus asked, you want to insist.
Jesus speaks again: 'Simon, are you fond of me?'
He's changed what he's asking.
He's met Simon where he is.

Simon sees John following at a distance. *'What about him?'*
Don't worry about him, Peter. Don't compare.
I'll meet you where you are, not where someone else is.

You look at your life.
The times you've looked for Jesus, waiting for him to meet you in your Sunday best, or when you behave exactly like the woman three pews down. Times when you put on a show of being sorted.

I'll meet you where you are . . .

You look at your life. It's full of pain, and struggle, and false comparisons.
That's where you are.
Jesus wouldn't want to be there.
And yet, **I'll meet you where you are.**

Will he? You wait, resisting the urge to change into your Sunday best.
Then you hear his whisper, inviting you to be real.
Are you fond of me?
He's met you where you are.

Look with my eyes. What do you see?

Met.

Father God, thank you that you meet me where I am. I don't have to be in a good place for you to meet me. Sometimes I am nervous about telling you where I am, even though you know. But, right now, I am in . . . Please meet me here. Amen.

GODLY

His divine power has given us everything we need for a godly life through our knowledge of him who called us by his own glory and goodness.

2 Peter 1:3

Today, I choose godliness.
Because godliness has been chosen for me,
godliness is possible.
The ability to live as God wants has been
placed within me.
I must believe that.

To doubt a truth is to believe a lie.

But the lie is more believable than the truth.
How can godliness be a part of who I'm created
to be?
God is so far above me
in every sense.
How can I begin to reach for what he wants,
let alone comprehend it?

I don't think I can.

And yet, godliness is a part of me now.
It's in there somewhere.
Always accessible.

God has promised.

I can be the person he made me to be.
Knowing him more as I learn more of him.
Pushing aside my doubts to reveal his truth.
Certain that
godliness is possible.

God has promised.

Because godliness has been chosen for me
today
I choose godliness.[1]

Look with my eyes. What do you see?

Godly.

Father God, it blows my mind that you make it possible for me to be godly. Help me choose to live a godly life, emulating and reflecting you, living as you want me to live. Amen.

GRACED

My grace is sufficient for you, for my power is made perfect in weakness.

2 Corinthians 12:9

Higher than the heavens,
you come down.

Down to this world.
Down to where we are.
Down to where I am.

And where I am is a long way down.

The ground beneath my feet crumbles
and I slip further
and further.

Yet you're there.
Always.

However low I go,
you're there.

'I can't do it any more,'
I whisper.
Thank you,
you say.

My pain and tear-filled eyes ask questions.
'Thank you?'
Thank you for allowing me to perfect my strength in you.

But I said I can't do it anymore.
I can't cope.
I'm not strong.

My child, you are never stronger than when you turn to me and say 'I can't'.[1]

Look with my eyes. What do you see?

Graced.

Father God, I can't. I can't do it. Thank you that you can, and will. Amen.

HOST

If anyone hears my voice and opens the door, I will come in and eat with that person . . .

Revelation 3:20

'It's not very tidy,' you say apologetically, but he doesn't seem to notice.
He strides in, giving you a hug as he passes.
You close the door and follow him.

He sits down at the dining table. **Let's eat.**
You remember when he fed a crowd with just a few loaves and fish.
Perhaps he's going to produce some food now.
You look at him, sitting at your table.
You remember what he said before he fed the crowd: 'You give them something to eat' (Matt. 14:16).
He nods gently. *You give them something to eat.*
Your mind runs through the contents of your pantry.
The out-of-date jars would be fine for you, but you can't give them to Jesus.
The bread is supermarket own brand; it can't compare to the bread Jesus produced. You wish you were one of those people who can whip up delicious scrambled eggs, but you're not. Even if you had eggs in.
You give them something to eat.
You give me something to eat.
Let's eat.

He's saying he wants what you can give.
He knows what's in your pantry.
You know he knows. **Let's eat.**
He's hungry for what you can offer him. **Let's.**

You go to the kitchen, and come back with supermarket bread, and jam that passed its sell-by date two weeks ago.
'Thank you,' he says. He's smiling as though you've laid a banquet before him, and you realise you have. You have given him a banquet.
You offer him some more.
He takes it.
And it dawns on you: you're hosting Jesus.

Look with my eyes. What do you see?

Host.

Father God, you know me, you know my resources. They often seem nothing to me; help me believe that they are a banquet to you and remember to offer them to you. Let's eat. Amen.

TREE

He is like a tree planted by streams of water . . .

Psalm 1:3, NIV 1984

At Christmastime, we children would put on a play for the adults, who always appeared enthralled, perhaps showing that they were the best thespians in the room.
One year, I had a starring role.
I was the tree.
More than that, I volunteered to be the tree.

Psalm 1 tells us that to have tree status, to be like a tree planted by a stream, is to know blessing.

Willow trees grow best near water, and may have been the trees referred to in Psalm 1.
Something about willows: apparently, they can talk to each other.
If willow number one gets attacked by webworms, it releases particular chemicals, sending a warning to willows number two plus.
The two plus group consequently protect themselves; they produce more tannin, making their leaves more difficult for pests to digest.

The trees are blessed by being planted by a stream, able to receive warning from others, and are a blessing by being able in turn to warn and protect.

Perhaps we could all volunteer to be a tree.

Volunteer to care enough about our fellow body of Christ members to warn them of things that might be damaging to their spiritual health.
Volunteer to have the grace to receive warnings from them.

Volunteer to release spiritual tannin, to pray for spiritual protection, and to hold on tight to God.
Volunteer to know blessing.

[Trees] put their roots deep into the ground and they hold on tight.
I can protect you from the storms that come your way.
You don't have to do it alone.
Root yourself deep in me.
And hold on tight.[1]

Look with my eyes. What do you see?

Tree.

Father God, I want to volunteer to know blessing and to be a blessing. Help me root myself in you. Amen.

79

WANTED

Father, if you are willing, take this cup from me; yet not my will, but yours be done.

Luke 22:42

Driving past olive groves in Corfu, I thought of Jesus.
It was on the Mount of Olives that Jesus prayed, 'I don't want to do this.'

I imagine many of us have been – perhaps are – in an 'I don't want to do this' place.
Let's know that Jesus understands.
He's been there.
'I don't want to do this . . .'
And his humanity meets God's sovereignty: '. . . but I want what you want more.'

Jesus wrestled to a position where he could say, 'Your will be done.'
Perhaps you need to wrestle to a 'Your will be done' position.
Let Jesus be your guide.

And what was God's will? What did God want?
He wanted you.
That's why Jesus needed to go to the cross; to open a way to God.
To forge the way of salvation.
God wanted you.

'Wanted posters' are put up when someone, or something, is lost and someone wants to find them. Often a reward is offered.

God held up a wanted poster with your picture on it.
Jesus saw that poster, and Jesus knew how to find you.

> By suffering, the servant will learn the true meaning of obeying the LORD. Although he is innocent, he will take the punishment for the sins of others, so that many of them will no longer be guilty.
>
> *Isa. 53:11, CEV*

He said, 'Your will be done' and he enabled it to happen.
Through his death and resurrection, he opened the way to God.
Jesus' reward for finding you is you.
God wants to share your company, your character, your life, your everything.
Will you let him?

What do you see? Look with my eyes.

Wanted.

Father God, thank you that there was a poster with my picture on it. Thank you for wanting me; company, character, life. When I feel that no one wants me, help me remember that you do. Thank you that Jesus said, 'Your will be done.' Amen.

TRAFFIC-LIGHTED

'The LORD is my shepherd . . . He makes me lie down in green pastures, he leads me beside quiet waters . . .

Psalm 23:1–2

'Make me' is often a defiant response to something one doesn't really want to do.
'I'll make you do it' is fairly threatening.
So it might be helpful to look at the meaning of 'makes me lie down'.
Is our Shepherd threatening us? Forcing us to get down?

'Makes lie down' is all one word in Hebrew, meaning to cause to rest.
Sheep sleep lying down. They may nap while standing, but real, restful sleep comes when they are lying down. And sheep only feel comfortable lying down if they feel safe.
So by making us lie down, our Shepherd is saying, **Stop. You're safe. You can relax. Rest in my green pastures.**
But I don't see any green pastures? Everything around looks stressful and bare.
Have a rest in my green pastures.
But I don't see any . . . **I'm here.**

Stopping can be scary. If we stop, maybe we'll never get going again.

The Lord, my Shepherd, makes me lie down in green pastures.
The Lord, my Shepherd, leads me beside quiet waters.

Lead here means to guide, to bring along.

Because the Lord is my Shepherd, he causes me to rest,
He brings me along and guides me beside resting places.

We will get going again, with him as our guide.
Trust your stopping and your waiting and your starting to me.
When we look to him, learning to hear our Shepherd's voice, we relax. We realise that we are not in charge, he is.
Like a heavenly traffic light, he directs us.
And we realise that, actually, that's rather nice.

Look with my eyes. What do you see?

Traffic-lighted.

Father God, please cause me to rest, and bring me along with you when I get going. Thank you that you direct my stopping and my starting and my going. You restore my soul. Amen.

81

UPHELD

For we do not have a high priest who is unable to empathize . . .
Hebrews 4:15, NIV

'Shut the door in front of you.'
For a week, those words were directed at me, each time I tried to board the bus.
The others in the group didn't like me. I knew they were getting at me.
It never occurred to me that they were getting at Jesus, too.

Saul went around persecuting Christians.
He threw them in jail.
He made their lives – if they stayed alive – more than miserable.
One day, Saul was on his way to Damascus, murder and/or imprisonment on his mind.
He'd find these Christians, these people who were not honouring God.
These people who believed Jesus was the Messiah. Ha.
Saul pressed on, intent on wiping out the Jesus-followers.
A bright light.
Saul falls to the ground.
Hears a voice: 'Why do you persecute me?'
Is this a trick? Are those Christians here?
There's no one there. No one other than God.
Saul realises that:

> 'Who are you, Lord?'
>
> *Acts 9:5*

I'm Jesus. You are persecuting, harassing, oppressing me.

What? No, he wasn't. It was Jesus-followers he needed to wipe out.
He wasn't doing anything to Jesus.
Why are you persecuting me?
Jesus stands in solidarity with his followers.
He knows our pain; he feels it.
This hurts me too.
'Who are you, Lord?'
I am Jesus. Anything my children go through, I go through with them.
Solidarity. *'Why are you persecuting me?'* **Me.**
He stands/sits/walks/runs with us.
Whatever we go through, we are not alone.
We'll face this together. Because we are in it together.
You're upheld. By me.

Look with my eyes. What do you see?

Upheld.

Father God, thank you that you are with me, supporting me, championing me, upholding me. You get it, even if no one else does. Help me to remember I'm not alone. Amen.

WISE

But the wisdom that comes from heaven is first of all pure; then peace-loving, considerate, submissive, full of mercy and good fruit, impartial and sincere.

James 3:17

'Make a wish!' people say, as the birthday person blows out the candles on their cake.
Who knows if the wish will come true or not.
What about when God says, 'make a wish'? That's different.

Solomon had succeeded his father as king.
Soon afterwards, Solomon had his 'make a wish' moment.
God appeared to him, and told him to ask for anything he wanted.
It was within God's power to grant Solomon's wish.

Imagine you are Solomon. What would you ask for?
My niece, when she was 4 or 5, would have asked for a unicorn. No question.
What would you ask for?

Solomon asked for wisdom. He looked at the life in which he found himself, and he felt inadequate. How was he to know how to rule and govern as king?
Give me wisdom.
And God said yes.
Moreover, God was pleased to give Solomon wisdom.
He was glad to make Solomon wise.
He was happy to equip Solomon for his life.

What would you ask for? As you look at the life you are living, what do you need?
Solomon asked for wisdom, or more specifically 'skill in life'.[1]

Skill to manage to live the life we have.

Perhaps we feel inadequate. Perhaps we feel unable. Perhaps we feel ill-equipped.

What would you ask God for?

Give me wisdom. Give me skill in life. Make me wise with your wisdom. Peace-loving, considerate, submissive, merciful, impartial, sincere, full of good fruit.

> The Lord was pleased that Solomon had asked for this. So God said to him . . .
> 'I will do what you have asked.'
>
> *1 Kgs 3:10–12a*

Look with my eyes. What do you see?

Wise.

Father God, give me wisdom. Wisdom from heaven. Wisdom that is pure, peaceful, considerate . . . wisdom like yours. Amen.

83

HOREBBED

The LORD said, 'Go out and stand on the mountain in the presence of the LORD, for the LORD is about to pass by.'

1 Kings 19:11

Heart pounding, Elijah collapses in the desert. He just wants to die.
And the angel of God meets him there.
Take a break, have some food, have a nap.
When you're at the end of your tether, let God meet you there.

Refreshed, Elijah carries on until he reaches Horeb, the mountain of God.
When he's safe in a cave, God gently speaks to him:
'What are you doing here, Elijah?' (v. 9b)
I've been really serving you, and everyone ignores me, and now Jezebel wants to kill me.
God replies by inviting Elijah into his presence.

Wind, earthquake, fire pass by but God's presence is not in those.
Perhaps they'd have been too much for Elijah right then.
God comes in a 'gentle whisper' (v. 12) and, because he is horebbed – wrapped in Horeb – Elijah hears the whisper that means God is there.

Have you heard that '**I'm here**' whisper?
Has your heart snuggled into Horeb, the mountain of God?

Elijah heard the whisper in a place that carried echoes.
It was at Horeb that Moses received the Ten Commandments: 'I am the LORD your God, who brought you out of Egypt, out of the land of slavery' (Exod. 20:2).
Elijah would have known that God brought the people out of Egypt.
He'd have known that God went with them.

The **I'm here** Presence-Whisper had been true, and it was true. So, from his horebbed place, Elijah believed that it *would* be true, and he stepped out in the presence of God.

Make time for Horeb.
Be horebbed.
Believe again in the presence of God.

Look with my eyes. What do you see?

Horebbed.

Father God, thank you for inviting me into your presence. May I always RSVP 'yes'. Help me snuggle into Horeb. When I am exhausted and at the end of my tether, and when I'm not, remind me that I am horebbed. Amen.

84

BAREFOOT

Worship the LORD in the splendour of his holiness . . .

Psalm 96:9

In Exodus 3, Moses has seen a bush that's not burning up.
He goes closer.
And God says, **Stop.**
You're on holy ground.
You don't need to get closer to the bush.
Instead, get closer to holy ground.
Closer to holiness.
Closer to me.

God shifts Moses' focus from the bush to the possibilities of where he is right now.
Do you have a 'bush'? Something that you are trying to get closer to?
Serving, working, parenting, promotion . . . There's nothing wrong with bushes.
But they can cause us to lose focus on now.
Maybe God also says to you, **Stop. Take time to be on holy ground.**
Take off your shoes, they're getting in the way.

In ancient Israel, footwear symbolised social status. Peasants went barefoot.
And God said to Moses, who had been raised in a palace, **Take off your shoes.**
Your status, your background, your 'what I can do' is getting in the way.

Moses steps out of his sandals, standing barefoot before God.
Bringing nothing but himself.

Later, God sends Moses back to the palace.
A place that he knows. A place he can navigate.
A place he is gifted and equipped for.
But first, Moses stands barefoot before God.
What he knows, his background, his training, his talents, fade in God's holiness.

Do you make time to stand barefoot before God?
For Moses, holy ground was preparation ground.
Standing barefoot readied him for the steps ahead.
Equipped him for the coming challenges.
When we stand with nothing but ourselves to give, we are in a place to give everything.

Look with my eyes. What do you see?

Barefoot.

Father God, thank you for bringing me to holy ground, and seeing me there, telling me to stop there for a while. Help me take off my shoes. My heart wants to be barefoot in your holiness. Amen.

85

DECREASING

I have come that they may have life, and have it to the full.
John 10:10

I realised that my life had a lot of gaps in it.
Literal ones from multiple tumour removals, and metaphorical ones.
There's a gap where my hearing used to be.
A gap where my ability to run, or walk with ease, used to be.
A gap where my concentration/memory levels used to be.
A gap where my smile used to be.

Perhaps there are gaps in your life, too.
Lost hopes, and dreams.
Frustrations (which I think could be known as 'peace-gaps').
Losing sight of yourself in busy-ness, a 'gap' where you used to be.
A difficult past.
A worrying future.
Life is full of gaps.

When I recognised my gaps, God asked me a question:
'What are you going to fill the gaps with?'
In my case, there were two options: bitterness, or God.

I began to invite God into my gaps, into my sadness at what I felt was missing.
John the Baptist, when he saw Jesus coming, said, 'He must become greater; I must become less' (John 3:30).
'Become greater' here carries the meaning of 'cause to grow'.[1]
As I invite God into my gaps, as he fills them, I – in a non-irreverent sense – 'cause him to grow' in my life.
And I see him more and more.
More of him, less of me.

I have a gap.
Bitterness is claiming it.
Elbowing its way in.
I can feel it.
Bitterness has very bony elbows.
I don't want it here.
It's not welcome.
I can't get rid of it.
I'll invite the One who can . . .

Look with my eyes. What do you see?

Decreasing.

Father God, God of my gaps, please fill me with yourself. I give my gaps to you. When I see a gap in my life, may I be reminded not of bitterness but of your *agapé* love in me. Amen.

86 RELEASED

Thanks be to God, who delivers me through Jesus Christ our Lord!

Romans 7:25

'My body's here, but I'm not.'
I'm 12 years old.
I've been denied my wish to stay at home while the rest of the family go to church, and my statement from the backseat of the car is the best I can do.
My body's here but I'm not.
I was separating the two.

At the end of Romans 7, Paul does similarly, speaking of God's law and sin's law.
His mind wants to follow God's law perfectly, but he finds himself unable to do so.

And what do we do when we are unable to follow God's ways perfectly every second of every day?
Shall we follow Paul's example, thank God for delivering us, and cut ourselves some spiritual slack?

In the fourteenth century, 'slack' meant to put an end to sorrow or hurts.
The phrase 'cut yourself some slack' refers to the loose part of a sail or rope, and means to give yourself a break. To be kind to yourself.

In striving to live as Christ would like, do we make space to also cut ourselves some slack? To loosen the pain our 'messing up' brings us, and release it to Jesus?

Remember that Jesus brings freedom from condemnation for those who are in him.[1]
We don't need to beat ourselves up.
Jesus took the beating for us.[2]
Could it be that when we beat ourselves up, we forget his work?

> As far as the east is from the west, so far has he removed our transgressions from us.
>
> *Ps. 103:12*

Let's throw away our beating-up-binoculars . . .

Look with my eyes. What do you see?

Released.

Father God, in striving for perfection, help me to remember grace. Your grace. The grace that sent Jesus for the times I mess up, and the grace that allows me to move on. Help me to accept it. I don't want to forget Jesus' work. Amen.

SHEPHERDED

I am the good shepherd; I know my sheep and my sheep know me . . .

John 10:14

What might those words have meant to Jesus' listeners?
What did it mean to be a shepherd in Jesus' day?

For some, it meant being the first to see and tell people about the Saviour of the world.[1] Jesus, the Good News, aligned himself with those who had told the world about him.

Shepherds were seen as untrustworthy.
By pronouncing himself the *good* shepherd, Jesus is showing a better way.

Sometimes, people in our lives let us down, or mistreat us.
Jesus says, **I'm not like that**.
Jesus is not people.

Perhaps it was hard to believe that a shepherd could be good. It was so ingrained in society that shepherds were *not* good.
Jesus was asking them to change their thinking, thinking that stemmed from experience.
I'm not like that.

Do you have thinking that stems from experience?
People always leave me. **I'm not like that. I'm your good shepherd.**
People laugh at me. **I'm not like that. I'm your good shepherd.**
People don't want to be my friend. **I'm not like that. I'm your good shepherd.**
People say I'm not good enough. **I'm not like that. I'm your good shepherd.**
I say I'm not good enough. **I'm not like that. I'm your good shepherd.**

Let me Shepherd you.
Follow me.
Listen to my voice and you'll learn to recognise it.
Let me lead you and protect you. Trust me.
I'm your good Shepherd.
Let me Shepherd you.

> He tends his flock like a shepherd: he gathers the lambs in his arms and carries them close to his heart . . .
>
> *Isa. 40:11*

Look with my eyes. What do you see?

Shepherded.

Father God, some 'shepherds' in my life are not good. Help me to truly know that you are not like them, you are not people, you care about me, you are my Good Shepherd. Thank you for shepherding me. Amen.

88

ALIVE

I have come that they may have life, and have it to the full.
John 10:10

Mount Moriah is the site of Abraham's testing[1] and of Jesus' crucifixion.

Moriah. That's where Abraham is headed.
Take your son, and sacrifice him at Mount Moriah.

Moriah. That's where God is headed.

> Without the shedding of blood, there is no forgiveness.
> *Heb. 9:22*

Moriah. That's where Abraham is headed.
'Where is the lamb?'
'God will provide the lamb.'

Moriah. That's where God is headed.
'Where is the lamb?'

> Look, the Lamb of God, who takes away the sin of the world!
> *John 1:29*

Moriah. That's where Abraham is.
Picking up a knife to kill his son.

Moriah. That's where God is.
Watching them nail his Son to a cross.[2]

Moriah. That's where Abraham is.
Hears **Stop!**
A ram instead.
Jehovah-Jireh: God will provide.

Moriah.
That's where God is.
Why?

> Why have you forsaken me?
>
> *Matt. 27:46*

Silence.
Jehovah-Jireh: God did provide.

> This is how much God loved the world: He gave his Son, his one and only Son. And this is why: so that no one need be destroyed; by believing in him, anyone can have a whole and lasting life.
>
> *John 3:16,* MSG

Look with my eyes. What do you see?

Alive.

Father God, thank you. Amen.

89

BALANCED

Who has measured the waters in the hollow of his hand, or with the breadth of his hand marked off the heavens? Who has held the dust of the earth in a basket, or weighed the mountains on the scales . . .?

Isaiah 40:12

'You have an unbalanced load,' said the engineer, peering at the washing machine.

An unbalanced load is when the washing is all squashed on one side of the drum, and stops the spin from working properly.

The way to sort it out is to stop the cycle, open the door, rearrange the washing so it is spread more evenly in the drum, shut the door, and put it on 'spin' again.

It got me thinking.

You have an unbalanced load.

Do I? Does the washing – the mix of thoughts and feelings and shapes and sizes and pressures and commitments and, and, and – inside me become all squashed in the wrong place and stop me working properly?

Stop me living as God intended me to live?

You have an unbalanced load.

I think I have.

Sometimes.

More than sometimes.

Stop. Open the door. Balance out the washing. Go again. Repeat as necessary.

Another thing I learned, as a budding washing machine expert, is that the load does not have to be unbalanced in the first place.

There is an optimum load which will never stop the spin from working properly.

The tricky thing is finding that optimum. It is different for every machine.
Every machine is made with the ability to work correctly.
Unhindered.
But it needs to be filled with the correct balance of things.

A load weighted, not a load weighed down.
A balanced load.
A 'working properly' load.
A load made easier simply because it is known . . .

Look with my eyes. What do you see?

Balanced.

Father God, please help me balance my life correctly. Let me recognise that my balance might look different from other people's, and that's OK. Amen.

90

CALM

But soon a fierce storm came up. High waves were breaking into the boat, and it began to fill with water.

Mark 4:37, ***NLT***

'It's getting a bit choppy,' Jesus' disciples may well have said, had they been British.
They were in the middle of storm.
Perhaps you, too, are experiencing a storm.

The disciples turn to Jesus, and find him asleep.
In the middle of their storm, Jesus is AWOL.
Perhaps you feel that.

They ask him, 'Don't you care that we're about to drown?' (v. 38).
Perhaps you're asking him that.
Don't you care?

Jesus cares. He knows that they won't drown.
He knows their storm. He knows your storm.
Jesus cares.
He speaks to storms. **Be still.**
Don't be agitated. Be calm.
And the storm obeys.

When all around is dark, I ask, where are you?
When everything in life is hard, where are you?
When I try until I cry
and need answers to my 'whys'
where are you?
My child, I'll never leave you, I'll never turn away.

I love you more than you can ever know.
In your darkness I'm your light,
When life's hard I'll be your strength.
When you try – you're not alone, I'm with you all the way.
I'm stronger than your fears,
I'm the one who'll dry your tears.
Your whys are in my hands – share them with me.
My child, I'll never leave you, I'll never turn away.
I love you more than you can ever know.

Look with my eyes. What do you see?

Calm.

Father God, thank you that you never really go AWOL. You're always here. May I share your voice? When you say 'Be still' to my storms, can I say it with you? Together? And then know calm again. Amen.

KEPT

Surely God is my help; the Lord is the one who sustains me.

Psalm 54:4

David and his men are one side of the mountain.
Saul and his men are the other.
Saul is trying to catch David, and David is trying desperately not to be caught.
I can imagine cartoon-makers having a field day with this!
But it's not a cartoon, it's real, and Saul is closing in.

Suddenly, a messenger arrives:

> Come quickly! The Philistines are raiding the land.
>
> *1 Sam. 23:27*

And Saul stops pursuing David, in order to deal with the Philistines.

Writing about this situation, in Psalm 54, David writes that God supported him, he could lean on God. God kept him going.
We might think it was the Philistines that saved David, really.
They stepped in at just the right moment.
But David credits his keeping to God.

> To him who is able to keep you from stumbling . . .
>
> *Jude 24*

More literally: to keep *from you* things that will make you stumble.[1]
What if we took that seriously?
God is able to 'keep from us' things that will cause us to fall.
May that encourage us, and strengthen our faith.
Something coming after us? Something closing in from the other side of the mountain?

We have a God who is able to keep us.
And who is able to keep the 'something' from causing us to fall.
A God who will help us.
A God who will sustain us.

When things press in – and they will – God says:
I've got you. You won't fall.
You're safe in my keeping.

Look with my eyes. What do you see?

Kept.

Father God, I often feel as though I am falling. Thank you that you won't let me fall. When things come at me, and make me wobble, help me remember that you are able to stop them from pushing me over. Amen.

92

CHERISHED

You keep track of all my sorrows. You have collected all my tears in your bottle. You have recorded each one in your book.

Psalm 56:8, NLT

This verse is not talking about happy tears.
It's talking about weeping.
The word used for 'bottle' is wineskin.
God collects our weeping tears in his wineskin.

In Bible times, water was generally not safe to drink.
It often carried disease, and pure water was often unavailable.
The people at the party had run out of wine, and Jesus stepped in to change that. He turned water into wine.[1]

My nephew collects badges. He's always on the lookout for them.

The first step in adding to his collection, is seeing a new badge.
The first step in God collecting our tears is seeing.
He sees them.

Next step is having a look at the badge. Assessing it. Getting to know it. God doesn't only see our tears, he knows them. He knows why we cry, perhaps even more than we know ourselves. He knows our inner hurts, and longings.

Next step is buying it.
Jesus bought our tears on the cross.
He took all our sadness and pain upon himself.
He said, **Those tears matter. They are worth dying for.**
If you are crying at the moment, tears on your face, or in your heart, or both, know that your tears matter to God.

Final step is pinning the badge with the rest of his collection, to keep it safe. Jesus collects our tears and, somehow, knowing that he does can make it better.
Water into wine.
In his safekeeping, in his trustworthiness, in his wineskin, the tears we cry are transformed.
They matter.
They are precious.
They are held.

Look with my eyes. What do you see?

Cherished.

Father God, thank you for collecting my tears. For making them matter. They don't need to be brushed away as insignificant, or unnecessary, or weak, because you see them as precious. Help me to do the same. Amen.

BLESSED

Why am I so honoured, that the mother of my Lord should visit me?
***Luke 1:43,* NLT**

When on a speaking engagement somewhere that has a first language other than English, I like to learn to say 'thank you' so I can thank people in their native tongue at the end.
One of the difficulties I find with learning new words, now I am deaf, is where to place the emphasis. I'm often unaware of emphasis.

Luke 1 is familiar, particularly read at Christmas, but I've never known a direct translation of Elizabeth's words read with the original emphasis:

How has it happened to *me* that the mother of my Lord should visit *me*?

Elizabeth is amazed by how blessed she is.
Blessed because Jesus is near.
He is near in Mary.

> I am with you always . . .
>
> *Matt. 28:20*

We know the blessing of having Jesus near, but what about the blessing of having him near in other people?
How often do we recognise that?

Seeing other people using their gifting.
Wow. Jesus is living in them, and I get to see it. Me! *I'm so blessed.*
Seeing people serving.
Wow. Jesus is living in them, and I get to see it. Me! *I'm so blessed.*
Someone offering to help.
Wow. Jesus is living in them, and I get to see it. Me! *I'm so blessed.*

Sometimes we can almost become entitled with regards to blessings.
We are so used to having so much, that we take it for granted.
We forget to 'count our blessings', including the blessing of having Jesus near in other people.

Do you use emphasis?
How has it happened to *me* that *I* should be so blessed?

Look with my eyes. What do you see?

Blessed.

Father God, thank you for blessing me so much. Please help me see you in other people, and recognise blessing, as Elizabeth did. Help me to use emphasis. Why am *I* so blessed? Amen.

94

BRAVE

Though the fig-tree does not bud and there are no grapes on the vines, though the olive crop fails and the fields produce no food, though there are no sheep in the sheepfold and no cattle in the stalls, yet I will rejoice in the LORD, I will be joyful in God my Saviour.

Habakkuk 3:17–18

Habakkuk longs for justice but it seems as though God is not listening.[1]
'What's going on, God?' Habakkuk complains.

Perhaps when we look around at the world, and at our own lives, we see injustice.
It's not fair. And God seems silent.
Let's be like Habakkuk, and dare to be honest and tell God.

God is listening. His response to Habakkuk is one of acknowledgement, and reassurance:

> The LORD is in his holy temple, let all the earth be silent before him.
>
> *Hab. 3:20*

The Lord **is** in his temple. He is.
Let all the earth be silent before him.

God has heard Habakkuk's worries. He's heard what's on his heart.
He's talked with Habakkuk about it.
And now he says, **All those worries and concerns? Let them be silent for a while. Focus on me. I'm in my temple. Look at my holiness.**

As Habakkuk focuses on God, he reaches an 'I will rejoice' place (Hab. 3:18). Nothing has actually changed, except Habakkuk's perspective.
God is God. And God brings joy.

Figs are full of essential nutrients. The fig tree is not flourishing. The essentials are not there. *And I will rejoice anyway.*
'Rejoicing anyway' takes courage. It takes determination.
The word 'joyful' here means 'the attitude and action of favourable circumstance'.[2]
Whatever else, I will remember that I am blessed.
My attitude will be full of blessing.
I will live blessed. God is with me, and that gives me joy.

Though everything is rubbish, I WILL rejoice in my God.
It's a choice. A brave choice.
Is it a choice you make?

Look with my eyes. What do you see?

Brave.

Father God, am I brave enough to choose joy? I want to be. Please help me rejoice. Even when things are hard, may I find your joy. Amen.

95

UNBROKEN

They will be his people, and God himself will be with them and be their God. 'He will wipe every tear from their eyes . . . I am making everything new!'

Revelation 21:1–5a

It slipped from my hand, landing on the floor.
And it broke.
The next day, the shop displayed a notice:
All Breakages Must Be Paid For.

Adam and Eve.
They ate from the tree.
A chasm formed.
A gap between them and God.
A broken space.

All Breakages Must Be Paid For.

Life in the chasm.
Struggles. Disunity. Suffering.

All Breakages Must Be Paid For.

From the cross.

> It is finished.
>
> *John 19:30*

Gone is the gap.

All Breakages Have Been Paid For.

Restoration.
Yet still we live in broken spaces.
Illness. Poverty. Overwhelm.

And Jesus is there. Bridging the gap. Filling the gap.

And one day, one day . . . 'I am making everything new!'
No more hurting places.
All Breakages Have Been Paid For.

What do you see? Look with my eyes.

Unbroken.

Father God, thank you for paying the price. You take all the broken pieces in me, and make them new. Help me to be patient. One day . . . Amen.

EAGLE

Those who hope in the LORD will renew their strength. They will soar on wings like eagles; they will run and not grow weary, they will walk and not be faint.

Isaiah 40:31

The word for 'strength' here is often used for physical ability.[1]
'Hope' is sometimes translated 'wait'.
Those who wait-in-hope on the Lord will renew their ability.

That's the prescription God gives us: wait-in-hope for him.
And as we do, waiting on his timing, hoping in his promises, we just might find ourselves soaring.
Moving from lower to higher.
From 'can't anymore' to 'can now'.
Like eagles.

Eagles are experts at being carried on the wind.
Sometimes, a feather will fall from one wing and the eagle will shed a feather from the other, to help them balance.
Shedding a feather seems a small thing, yet it's vital if they are to soar.
Eagles are so in tune with their bodies.

What about us?
When we've waited-in-hope, are we aware of things that may be adversely affecting us? Things that are unhelpful in our relationship with God?
A feather falling out, causing us to wobble.

God has promised that we will – and therefore can – soar on wings as eagles.
A wobble is not the end of the world.
We just need to make sure we shed whatever 'feather' is hindering our progress, stopping us from soaring higher.
And we can do that.
After all, God has said we will soar like eagles.

Perhaps there's a reason 'soaring' comes before 'running' and 'walking'.
Running and walking are active whereas soaring, for the most part, is passive.
Being comes before doing.
If we want to 'do', then we first need to learn to 'be'.
To wait-in-hope. To be renewed.
Like eagles.

What do you see? Look with my eyes.

Eagle.

Father God, please help me recognise when a feather falls out, so that I can be renewed. Help me to wait-in-hope. I'm looking forward to soaring again. Amen.

97

STANDING

Put on the full armour of God, so that when the day of evil comes, you may be able to stand your ground, and after you have done everything, to stand.

Ephesians 6:13

It's an honour to be a priest.[1]
I've never thought otherwise.
Even now, as I stand on dry ground in the middle of the Jordan.

I wasn't sure what would happen when Joshua passed on the message from God to us priests: 'Go and stand in the river' (Josh. 3:8).
Right now, the Jordan is in flooding season, but we held onto the ark of the covenant we were carrying in a box, poles across our shoulders, and walked to the river.
The water stopped flowing!
We walked on dry ground to the middle of the riverbed, and stood there.
We are still standing there.
People are hurrying past, crossing over as we stand.

I think of my priestly duties: presenting offerings, looking after God's sanctuary.
Such special things to do. Such vital things to do.
And yet, as I stand here, I feel a new sense of awe.
A realisation that my calling culminates in this: to stand.
If I don't stand, we won't reach the Promised Land. We'll drown.

Glancing down at the dry riverbed, my eyes skim over my robes.
Priestly garments. Clothes that show who I am.
I stand here in who I am.
A child of God.
Called to stand.

Normally I'd be offering sacrifices now.
That's my calling, too.
But not right now.
For now, I'm called to stand.

I straighten my back, gripping the pole resting on my shoulder.
The water is held back.
People walk by.
God is in charge.

And I stand.

What do you see? Look with my eyes.

Standing.

Father God, help me make time to stand in your presence. Stand on your Word. Stand as I am. I do sometimes feel as though I am sinking. If I don't stand, I'll drown. Help me stand my ground. Help me stand your ground. Please remind me to stand. Amen.

98

EBENEZERED

Then Samuel took a stone and set it up between Mizpah and Shen. He named it Ebenezer, saying, 'Thus far the LORD has helped us.'

1 Samuel 7:12

God has just helped the Israelites beat the Philistines.
Samuel sets up a stone, and calls it 'Ebenezer'.
It was a reminder of a God who helps.
Anyone who saw that stone, whatever their current circumstances, would be reminded of Ebenezer God.

It was an encouragement to look back, and be reminded of God's faithfulness.
God helped them before, and God doesn't change. Ebenezer God.

As you look back at your life, can you see Ebenezer God moments?

I was on a busy train. Someone offered me their seat. *Ebenezer God.*

I was in Intensive Care. Slowly I recovered. *Ebenezer God.*

People are kind. *Ebenezer God.*

As I learn to recognise Ebenezer God in all aspects of my life, I see his faithfulness.
And I begin to anticipate his constancy.

Nervous about tomorrow? Ebenezer God will be there.
Excited about tomorrow? Ebenezer God will be there.

Ebenezer God: our God who helps.

Every second of every day, he's there.
We're not managing things alone.
Help is literally at hand.
We're Ebenezered.

What do you see? Look with my eyes.

Ebenezered.

Father God, Samuel had a good idea. Sometimes I forget to turn to you for help; I know you always want to help me, yet I forget. Help me, especially in moments when I am so caught up in doing and keeping going, to bring you in. Amen.

99

VALUABLE

And when she finds it, she calls her friends and neighbours together and says, 'Rejoice with me; I have found my lost coin.'
Luke 15:9

I should have stopped rolling.
Why didn't I just lie down?
A tiny part of me wondered what it would be like to be away from the others.
Now I know, and I wish I didn't know.

I can see them from here.
I'm half hidden by a water jar, but I can see them.
At first, they seemed to miss me. 'Where's number seven?' they said.
But now they've stopped asking.
They are just getting on with life as a group of nine.
The only thing that's different is the woman.
She keeps turning on lamps and looking for something.

I don't know what she's looking for, as she sweeps and sweeps.
She only pauses to count the coins.
'... nine.' She dabs at her eyes.
'... nine.' She turns up the lamp.
'... nine.' She sweeps.
Even she is getting used to nine.

The brush sweeps near me, and I try to roll towards it.
Maybe if she sees me, she'll remember me.
But now I can't even start rolling.
'... nine.'
She shakes her head.

The brush sweeps near me again.
I don't even try to roll.
The brush stills, discarded.
Her hand reaches towards me,
picking me up, holding me aloft.
Holding me safe.
She dances with joy.

She was looking for me.

What do you see? Look with my eyes.

Valuable.

Father God, thank you for not giving up on me. I'm so glad you found me. Thank you for dancing with joy, and for holding me safe. Amen.

CONTENT

'For I know the plans I have for you,' declares the LORD, 'plans to prosper you and not to harm you, plans to give you hope and a future.'

Jeremiah 29:11

'What's the plan?' is a bit of a catchphrase of mine.
I like to have things in the diary, knowing the anticipation of promised dates and events.

Way back, even before God made the world, he had an answer to 'what's the plan?' and his answer was 'you'.

I find it incredible that God planned me in.
I'm not here by accident; wasn't a spur-of-the-moment thing.
There are times in my life when I wish he hadn't bothered.
Times when I certainly wouldn't plan myself in.
Yet God did.

Did he do so with a sense of anticipation?
Some translations have 'thoughts' instead of 'plans'.
God thinks of us, and our prospering: our well-being, our contentment, our safety.
He's planned ahead for it.
He's written it in.
Which means it's possible.

We can be content.
It's in his diary for us.
Will we meet him there?
Will we align our plans with his and meet him in content?

‘What’s the plan?’

I have a tough day ahead. **I know.**

I’m not looking forward to it. **No.**

You know that thing you said about planning for my contentment? **Yes.**

Did you miss out today? **No.**

So, even today, I can be content? **Yes.**

How? **Come on, I’ll show you . . .**

> I have learned to be content whatever the circumstances.
>
> *Phil. 4:11*

What do you see? Look with my eyes.

Content.

Father God, thank you for planning for my contentment. That means I can be content, but I’m not always. Teach me your plans. Show me, every day. Help me learn to be content, no matter what. Guide me to find my contentment in you. Amen.

INCLUDED

I say to the Lord, 'You are my Lord; apart from you I have no good thing.'

Psalm 16:2

'Can I play/come/watch?' Children often ask this, meaning, *Can I be included?*

Perhaps as Christians we ask God the same thing:
Can I be included?
Can I be included in joy, in love, in peace, in strength . . . ?

'Can I be included?' is a vulnerable question.
It risks the answer being no.
Except, with God, it doesn't.

As Paul wrote: 'you are the body of Christ, and each one of you is a part of it' (1 Cor. 12:27).
You are included, whether you feel it or not.
You don't need to stand on the outside looking in, because you are a part of it.
Filling a space in the body of Christ that only you can fill.

Can I be included?
You already are.
Will you let yourself be included?

> Every good and perfect gift is from above, coming down from the Father of the heavenly lights, who does not change like shifting shadows.
>
> *Jas 1:17*

Every good thing comes from God. Where there is good, there is God. Do we sometimes wonder if we can be included in 'good'?

My niece likes gymnastics. After her first competition, she sat down. Then she stood up again, her face alight with wonder: 'They said my name!' and she went to receive her prize.

> And now the prize awaits me – the crown of righteousness, which the Lord, the righteous Judge, will give me on the day of his return. And the prize is not just for me but for all who eagerly look forward to his appearing.
>
> *2 Tim. 4:8, NLT*

May our faces light up with wonder:
He said my name.

What do you see? Look with my eyes.

Included.

Father God, thank you for including me. Including me in good. Including me in where you are. Including me in you. Thank you for saying my name. Amen.

Isaiah 43:1–4a

But now, this is what the LORD says –
he who created you, Jacob,
he who formed you, Israel:

'Do not fear, for I have redeemed you;
I have summoned you by name; you are mine.

When you pass through the waters,
I will be with you;
and when you pass through the rivers,
they will not sweep over you.

When you walk through the fire,
you will not be burned;
the flames will not set you ablaze.

For I am the LORD your God,
the Holy One of Israel, your Saviour;
I give Egypt for your ransom,
Cush and Seba in your stead.

Since you are precious and honoured in my sight,
and because I love you . . .

Notes

1 Shielded

[1] https://strongsconcordance.org/results.html?k=shield (accessed 19 January 2025).

2 Strong

[1] Phil. 4:13.
[2] See Judg. 16:28.

5 Uninterrupted

[1] Heb. 7:21.
[2] Heb. 7:2.
[3] Isa. 9:6.

7 Beloved

[1] Gen. 17:17–18.
[2] E.g. Deut. 33:12.

8 Hidden

[1] Gen. 3:11.

9 Praiser

[1] Neh. 8:10.

11 Still

[1] Based on Ps. 46:10.

13 Able

1 *Chariots of Fire*, distributed by 20th Century Fox, The Ladd Company Warner Bros., 1981.

16 Loved

1 Mark 10:13.
2 John R. Kohlenberger III, *NIV Exhaustive Concordance* (Grand Rapids, MI: Zondervan 1999), p. 1523, ref. 26.

19 Image-bearer

1 Esth. 4:11.

20 Recognised

1 Pigs were 'unclean' to Jews, see Lev. 11:7.

23 Lit

1 Gen. 1:3.
2 John 8:12.

24 Equipped

1 1 Kgs 17:9.
2 1 Kgs 17:13–16.

25 Poeima

1 https://www.azquotes.com/quote/1458906 (accessed 29 January 2025).

27 Righteous

1 Isa. 61.
2 See Exod. 14; Exod. 17.

28 Peace-full

1 Luke 15:22.

29 Shiny

[1] Based on Roger Hargreaves, *Mr Grumpy* (London: Farshore Books, 2018). See https://www.youtube.com/watch?v=M0VaGhf3dio (accessed 3 February 2025).

[2] https://www.blueletterbible.org/lexicon/g185/niv/mgnt/0-1/ (accessed 19 January 2025).

34 Accepted

[1] John 2:24.

[2] John 3:1–21.

35 Forgiven

[1] Matt. 26:74.

[2] John 21.

36 Joy-full

[1] Quotations taken from *Still Emily* by Emily Owen 2016, published by Sarah Grace Publishing, an imprint of Malcolm Down Publishing.

38 Holy

[1] Quotations taken from *Still Emily* by Emily Owen 2016, published by Sarah Grace Publishing, an imprint of Malcolm Down Publishing.

39 God's Place

[1] 2 Chr. 5.

41 Unveiled

[1] Exod. 34:29–35.

42 Ambassador

1 Attributed to Teresa of Avila, https://www.journeywithjesus.net/poemsandprayers/3637-Teresa_Of_Avila_Christ_Has_No_Body (accessed 14 January 2025).

43 Salt

1 Lev. 2:13.

45 Special Possession

1 Isa. 43:1.

47 Habited

1 Kohlenberger, *NIV Exhaustive Concordance*, p. 1568, ref. 3443.

50 Hands-full

1 Exod. 4:1.
2 Exod. 4:2.
3 Kohlenberger, *NIV Exhaustive Concordance*, p. 1542, ref. 1466.

52 Covered

1 Song 2:4.

55 Seen

1 Emily Owen, *God's Calling Cards* (Milton Keynes: Authentic Media, 2019), p. 38.

56 Home

1 Based on Luke 15:11–32.

57 Accompanied

1 Luke 2:49.

59 Empowered

[1] Acts 2:1–15.

60 Beautiful

[1] See NIV 1984.

61 Welcome

[1] Gal. 2:20.

65 Close

[1] Matt. 17:1–13.
[2] Matt. 26:36–46.

67 New

[1] Luke 8:2.

69 Kind

[1] https://www.ons.gov.uk/peoplepopulationandcommunity/crimeandjustice/articles/homicideinenglandandwales/yearendingmarch2023 (accessed 17 January 2025).
[2] From NIV 1984.
[3] See Josh. 2.
[4] Adapted from Emily Owen, *The Power of Seven* (Milton Keynes: Authentic Media, 2018), p. 46.

70 Valued

[1] Lev. 14:1–7, https://biblehub.com/commentaries/ellicott/leviticus/14.htm (accessed 19 January 2025).

71 Rester

[1] Kohlenberger, *NIV Exhaustive Concordance*, p. 1528, ref. 398.

72 Royal

[1] Mark 3:34–35; Rom. 8:29; Heb. 2:11; 1 John 3:2.

75 Godly

[1] Owen, *The Power of Seven*, p. 168.

76 Graced

[1] Owen, *God's Calling Cards*, p. 72.

78 Tree

[1] Owen, *The Power of Seven*, p. 15.

82 Wise

[1] Kohlenberger, *NIV Exhaustive Concordance*, p. 1404, ref. 2683.

85 Decreasing

[1] https://www.blueletterbible.org/lexicon/g837/niv/mgnt/0-1/ (accessed 19 January 2025).

86 Released

[1] Rom. 8:1.

[2] E.g. John 19:1.

87 Shepherded

[1] Luke 2:8–20.

88 Alive

[1] Gen. 22.

[2] Matt. 27:35.

91 Kept

[1] Kohlenberger, *NIV Exhaustive Concordance*, p. 1602, ref. 5875.

92 Cherished

[1] John 2:1–12.

94 Brave

[1] Hab. 1:1–2.
[2] Kohlenberger, *NIV Exhaustive Concordance*, p. 1385, ref. 1635.

96 Eagle

[1] Kohlenberger, *NIV Exhaustive Concordance*, p. 1423, ref. 3946.

97 Standing

[1] Josh. 3.

www.ingramcontent.com/pod-product-compliance
Lightning Source LLC
LaVergne TN
LVHW010613100826
845148LV00014B/2946

* 9 7 8 1 7 8 8 9 3 4 3 7 4 *